THE GOSPEL OF THE
KINGDOM

Books by Frederick C. Grant

The Economic Background of the Gospels

The Life and Times of Jesus

The Early Days of Christianity

The Way of Peace: Devotional Addresses

New Horizons of the Christian Faith

The Growth of the Gospels

Form Criticism: A New Method of New Treatment Research, by Rudolf Bultmann and Karl Kundsin (*translated*)

The Beginnings of our Religion (*edited*)

Frontiers of Christian Thinking

The History of Primitive Christianity, by Johannes Weiss (*translated and edited*)

The Message of Jesus Christ, by Martin Dibelius (*translated*)

The Gospel and the Predicament of Modern Man (*edited*)

The Basic Formula for Church Union (*co-author*)

THE GOSPEL OF THE KINGDOM

FREDERICK C. GRANT

THE HASKELL LECTURES 1940

NEW YORK

THE MACMILLAN COMPANY

1940

To My Son

Robert McQueen Grant

Companion in Many Studies

PREFACE

The principles of modern New Testament criticism are not different from those which have proved fruitful in other fields, for example in the study of the Old Testament and the History of Religions. In these fields the most productive method has been the study of historical background and social environment: a capital illustration of the value of this method is the modern interpretation of the Old Testament prophets. In the New Testament these principles ought to be applied with the same thoroughness and at the same time with the same care and discrimination with which they are applied in those other fields. However, it often happens, no doubt as a consequence of the central importance of the New Testament for Christian faith, that critics who do not hesitate to apply fully the methods of historical and literary criticism to the Old Testament, to Church History, and to History of Religions, do hesitate when they come to the New Testament; some even insist that although literary, historical, and form criticism may properly be applied to the Old Testament, say to Isaiah, Genesis, or Deuteronomy, nevertheless when we come to the New Testament the gospels 'must be taken as they stand'. But such a position is completely untenable, and, as I hope to show in the pages that follow, the gains not only to historical knowledge but also to faith far outweight the losses; and those gains lie on the other side of the risks involved in the process, and cannot be attained by some short-cut which would isolate or insulate the earliest Christian tradition from the fullest, frankest kind of literary, textual, historical, philological, and tradition criticism.

The purpose of this book is to set forth and discuss the new approach to the life and teaching of Jesus, chiefly his Gospel of the Kingdom, and to the origin of Christianity which results from a fuller application of the methods of historical and literary research to the tradition underlying the gospels. If it makes any contribution whatever to the subject, it is probably by way of a fresh study of the environment and background of the Gospel. Too often the methods adopted in studying the teaching of Jesus have been purely exegetical. Modern ideas have been read-in between the lines. Or ancient Jewish apocalyptic has been made the key to unlock the whole 'mystery of the Kingdom'—this method has been in vogue chiefly since the recovery and popularization of the Jewish and early Christian pseudepigraphic literature during the opening years of the present century, or rather between 1890 and 1914.

Much recent theology has been milling about in a cul-de-sac, as far as the New Testament is concerned, owing to the vast over-emphasis upon apocalyptic eschatology in interpreting the origins of Christianity and especially the teaching and career of Jesus. The situation goes back to the rise of 'thorough-going eschatology' about 1900, and chiefly to Schweitzer's *Quest of the Historical Jesus* (published in Germany 1906; English translation 1910). It is the fundamental insincerity of 'thorough-going eschatology' that is at fault. The 'eschatologists' knew as well as anyone that the gospel sources are not on

one level, that Matthew depends upon Mark, that John is
later in development and point of view and probably in
time than the Synoptics; but they suppressed all this, and
instead preferred to pick and choose—chronology from
Matthew and John, 'Son of Man' theology from Matthew,
the concept of the Judgment from the Synoptic Apocalypse, and so on. They succeeded in impressing modern
theological readers, thanks to a similar and widespread
confusion of thought, viz. the assumption that criticism
has no secure and recognized foundations, that it may be
ignored in the pulpit, that exegesis does not depend upon
historical or literary interpretation but is guided by some
kind of intuitive faculty superior to knowledge and reason. The 'eschatologists' were playing with ideas—as Ph.D.
candidates at German universities often did, before the
War. Take an idea and see what you can make of it!
Shuffle the cards once more and deal yourself a new soli-
taire hand! Scramble the jig-saw pieces! Leave out this
factor and add that, and see if you cannot find a new and
workable formula! But history requires *all* the factors. We
have none too many, and are not helping the case by sup-
pressing some of them.

Those who thought Harnack's interpretation of the
Gospel of Jesus too academic, too 'liberal', too 'reduced' in
its Christology, seized upon 'thorough-going eschatology'
as a new revelation. The Abbé Loisy and Father Tyrrell
saw in it a guarantee and support of Catholic supernaturalism; and many who were not supernaturalists but had been
reading R. H. Charles's translations of the apocryphal and
pseudepigraphic writings felt themselves persuaded that
here was sound historical interpretation. (No one doubted

that the apocalypses represented average, everyday Judaism, and that all Jews of the first century retired each night hopeful that the morrow would bring the Day of Judgment!) But Catholic supernaturalism needed no such flimsy support: Von Hügel's *Essays* pointed to a firmer foundation, viz. the life in grace of the saints. This should have meant something to Protestantism. One wonders why it did not mean more. And in the second place, we now know considerably more about first-century Judaism, thanks very largely to the late George Foot Moore, whose *Judaism in the First Centuries of the Christian Era* (1927) is already a classic of scholarship, and to the colossal *Commentary on the New Testament from Talmud and Midrash* of Hermann Strack and Paul Billerbeck (1922-1928).

Perhaps the most devastating consequence of 'thoroughgoing eschatology' is that it opened the door to Barthianism, with its monstrous misinterpretation of the Gospel, its Marcionite or Manichean Unknown God of force and terror, its purely transcendental Christ, its Kingdom completely 'not of this world'. For all the criticisms levelled against it, Ritschlianism was certainly a fairer interpretation of historical Christianity and of the Gospel of Jesus than this bizarre system, which undercuts all Christian motivation toward social righteousness, denies the fundamental postulate of the Gospel, viz. that the Kingdom is coming in this world, and opens upon a dark cloudland of impressive but vague and barbarous and incomprehensible ideas set forth in completely arbitrary terminology.

What I have tried to do is to see the movement of primitive Christianity as a whole and against its total background, political and economic as well as religious (the three are never separable, except for discussion). And I have preferred to see the gospel tradition in the light of its earliest Jewish environment rather than in the light of later ecclesiastical interpretations, chiefly Hellenistic or Graeco-Roman. The result is a picture of Jesus as a prophet and a teacher—but one who was 'more than a prophet' and certainly one who taught 'not as the scribes'—rather than as a social reformer, the 'founder' of a religious movement, an ethical philosopher, or a fanatical apocalyptist. All these interpretations owe something to his teaching, seize upon and elaborate one or another element in its manifold variety; but none of them, nor all of them taken together, suffice to account for him. After all, Jesus was unique, and does not fit any specified category, ancient or modern. And his Gospel, though not a pattern of an ecclesiastical system nor yet a program for modern social reform, is still 'social' through and through—social *because* religious, in the ancient biblical understanding of religion.

It is the thesis of this book that the movement headed by Jesus of Nazareth was much more widespread than the gospels represent; their interests are those of the church of their time, and their method is selective; they are concerned with the apostles and their relations to Jesus more than with the response of the multitudes to his ministry and message. Not only was the movement which marked 'the beginning of the gospel' more widespread than the evangelic records suggest but it was recognized from the first to have a 'social' import. But it was not one more *neoterism* or threat of revolution of the kind Josephus so frequently describes and condemns. Jesus took for granted

the Old Testament or prophetic conception of the Kingdom (rather than the apocalyptic) as the Reign of God,
centered in the theocracy but extending to the ends of the
earth. By its very nature the idea forbade the inferences
of Zealots and revolutionists: God is already King, and his
Reign cannot be set up by men. Jesus' conception of the
Kingdom of God was centered in his conception of God as
King, i.e. as Father. It was something more than a theodicy,
or a philosophy of history. Semitic thought was not philosophical in the first century nor for long after. The conception was derived from the Old Testament, not from
the apocalypses nor from the legal tradition of the scribes.
Though both the apocalypses and the legal tradition depended likewise upon the Old Testament, the relation
of the Gospel to it was more direct and central than that
of either of the other two types of thought.

God's Kingdom is everlasting. Even the apocalypses
acknowledge this: e.g. the Book of Daniel, which represents the Kingdom as *coming,* and yet insists in the strong-
est language that the Kingdom of the Most High is eternal,
that is 'everlasting' (7:27). But not all things are now
subject to the Reign of God, though it be 'eternal in the
heavens'. Hence the Kingdom must 'come', and is coming,
is about to come, is almost here, has already begun to
arrive: ἤγγικεν ἡ βασιλεία τοῦ θεοῦ. Its realization does
not depend upon men, since it already exists; and yet the
one rebellious province must be reconquered and reincorporated in the empire, that God may be 'all in all'. Hence
the best definition of the Kingdom is the liturgical one:
"Thy Kingdom come, thy will be done on earth as it is in
heaven."

Jesus' ethics are not a preliminary announcement of the law which is to obtain in some apocalyptic 'Kingdom' when it finally descends to earth, nor yet the rules which are to govern the conduct of his followers during the interval until that blessed day arrives. On the contrary his teaching is the further exposition, the 'fulfilment' of the ancient theocratic Law which had been 'given to those of old time' and really rested upon the purpose and intention of the Creator of the world. Hence Jesus' criticism of the current interpretation of the Law, and even of the Law itself where it failed to measure up to the intention of the divine Lawgiver. The chief criticism was the old, perennial, prophetic one: both in idea and in practice the Law was irreformable. One code had been added to another, one interpretation to another, until the intention of the Lawgiver was obscured and in effect defeated. His criticisms centered very largely upon the provisions regarding property (corban, the tithe, etc.) and human rights (divorce, Sabbath, ablutions, etc.). The same problems still exist: How can new conditions and insights be met by any law? Law proverbially and inevitably falls short of the highest conceptions of human duty and opportunity, and by its very lag behind the highest idealism permits its own abuse. Today, for example, even the Christian law of marriage may be exploited and made to defeat the spirit back of enlightened legislation—ultimately the spirit of Christ—quite as readily as property law may be exploited by those who are determined to use it for their own ends and to evade the real purpose of its provisions. Law therefore is not an adequate category for describing the Gospel. Though Jesus took for granted the revelation in Torah, he went beyond it, not rejecting it but insisting upon a fulfilment of its requirements which exceeded all thought of minimums and rose to the loftier motive of perfect obedience to the will, the purpose, the intention of God.

Again, his conception of society is the old theocratic one, freed from its antiquated nationalistic limitations. It does not envisage a separation of state and church, say on the basis of divided loyalties as between Caesar and God, which—despite the scholastic attempt at a synthesis—is the mediaeval idea and the one to which our modern world has fallen heir and has now pushed to a further extreme. Upon our view the division is simply inevitable, in any pagan or half-pagan society; it was so for Augustine, and Dante, and the Holy Roman Empire (that is in practice, apart from theory), and it is so still. Under present conditions in the world, church and state must be separated; but the ideal is surely something different, viz. a state which is also a church. And this is the old Jewish theocratic conception, fundamental to all ancient Jewish history—certainly from the period of the Exile. There were objections to it, e.g. in Maccabean times (I Macc. 1:11), and there are still drawbacks to any such conception, the world being what it is. But the idea, as stated by the noblest of Old Testament prophets and reaffirmed and reënforced by Jesus, is not that of an exclusive Judaism (however necessary in practice that exclusive attitude was at one time) but the prophetic ideal of a world-state in which all men will know and worship the true God and live as brothers, all mankind one, with freedom and justice for all nations, the true *Civitas Dei,* the true Federation of the World. And that ideal is possible only on a religious basis, not one of clever statecraft or of pure human self-interest, however enlightened. Jesus' conception of the Kingdom of God is absolutely and unequivocally and exclusively a religious conception: purely and simply religious, but religious in the sound ancient sense, as embracing all of life, society, politics, the labor of men, as well as their inner feelings, attitudes, and aspirations.

The world in which Jesus lived was by no means the gay, carefree, idyllic Palestine of Renan's picturesque and romantic *Life of Jesus*, with its happy, industrious Galileans rejoicing in their daily toil, prospering upon a fertile, prolific land, each village family happy under its own vine and fig tree, the fishers on the lake singing as they drew in their teeming nets, and festal throngs setting forth on periodic pilgrimage to the sacred city in the southern highlands. No; it was a troubled world, more like the one we know; with the threat of political destruction hanging over it, a universal sentence of death pronounced against it; earnestly, desperately looking for salvation, by human power or divine, and ready to listen to anyone who promised a way out of or around the impending chaos and who could prove by tangible and unquestionable signs that his message was authentic. It was a distracted, enervated, harassed generation (Matt. 9:36), peevish and petulant as tired children (Matt. 11:15-17), and all but exhausted and despairing of any divine response.

In facing the disasters which threatened his people, Jesus at least proved that men can endure such prospects if their hearts are firm through faith in God: and if so, no external threats need daunt them. This much, at least, he proved—and this is his asceticism, his inner victory, his good cheer, having overcome the world (John 16:33). But his Gospel was more than that, and concerned the salvation not only of the private individual in a world threatened with doom, but of society itself, men generally, the world which stood under that threat.

We wish to know of course if Jesus was a pacifist, and if his Gospel involves that principle. It is certainly true that under the circumstances in first century Palestine no other course lay open to any person but a wild fanatic. And Jesus flatly rejected the Zealot program—he who by the irony of human fate was to be crucified as an insurrectionist! But does it follow that pacifism is the only true expression of the spirit of Christ? Under other circumstances, in a free nation, responsible for the maintenance of law and order and for the establishment of justice as well as for the maintenance of peace, the situation has been completely changed. 'Pacifism' invites aggression rather than checks it—as the history of Europe and Asia during the past decade amply proves. And Christ is 'the Son of Eternal Justice', as the Roman Pontiff stated in a recent address. This is a new title for him, to Protestant ears, but one that merits much pondering.

The order of the chapters is not chronological; what they are meant to set forth is not a history but the exposition of a view and an argument for the truth of that view. Chapter V might seem more appropriately to come first, and Chapter I later; but I have preferred to introduce the material where it seemed relevant to the argument, and where the student would find it useful in following the argument. A few selected titles of books and articles have been added in the Notes and References for the benefit of those who would pursue the subject further. The subject not only deserves that further study, but will endlessly enrich all who pursue it.

The Haskell Lectureship was founded in 1905 by the bequest of Mrs. Caroline E. Haskell of Chicago to provide an annual series of lectures on some phase of the influence of Christianity on the life and religion of the Near and Middle East. The lectures are given in the Graduate School of Theology, Oberlin College. The present series was delivered February 19-28, 1940.

CONTENTS

CHAPTER I

THE JESUS OF HISTORY

The earliest explanation of the rise of Christianity to be found in the pages of secular history is the oft-quoted passage in the fifteenth book of the *Annals* of Tacitus. It occurs in the course of that historian's account of the great fire at Rome in the year 64, an account (*Annals* xv. 38-44) which should be read in full. It was the worst conflagration Rome had ever suffered; it continued for over a week, and when the fire was at last put out more than three-fourths of the city lay in ruins.

Of the fourteen quarters into which Rome is divided, four only were left intact, three were burned to the ground, while in the remaining seven only a few relics of houses were left, broken and half-burned (§ 40).

Some persons ascribed the calamity to chance (§ 38). Others ascribed it to the hand of fate (§ 41), since it fell at an interval after the burning of Rome by the Gauls exactly equivalent to that between the founding of the city and the Gallic invasion; [1] and even the month and the day were the same, July 19. Still others found the cause in the execrable vanity and ambition of Nero; for the emperor wished, they said, to rebuild the city upon a more magnificent plan, including a great palace and grounds for his own use. Evidence of his guilt was seen in his continued absence, during the greater part of the week of horror, at Antium—he had not returned until the palace itself was threatened. Further, a report circulated that Nero had climbed a tower on the nearby house of Maecenas and there, arrayed in an appropriate theatrical costume and accompanying himself on the harp,[2] he had sung the destruction of Troy. And it was a fact that incendiaries, who were thought to be only carrying out the emperor's orders, had repulsed those who tried to stop the advance of the fire, and had indeed heaped fuel on the flames. Tacitus may be unfair to Nero, and to all the emperors down to Nerva. But he is not likely to be manufacturing the rumors he records. There was an undercurrent of opposition to the new dictatorship of the Caesars, which persisted throughout the first century; it was not limited to the fickle, irresponsible populace, but included men of intelligence and position who, although they probably recognized the futility of any hope of restoring the republic, nevertheless took their lives in their hands, from time to time, in order to oppose the ever-increasing tyranny. It is not Tacitus's own experience of this tyranny in its latest phase, which has prejudiced his record of the early empire; the sources which he is using are already permeated with criticism of the unbridled license and lust for power of the Julians, the Flavians, and their satellites. Among the early emperors none offered a more monstrous or more horrible example than Nero.

The fire having been finally put out and a plan for the

rebuilding of the city drawn up by the emperor's surveyors and architects—the promptness of the plan was another ground for suspicion—"the next care was to propitiate the gods" (§ 44). The Sibylline books were consulted; a band of matrons offered their prayers and sacrifices to Juno; the statues of the gods were laid in their beds amid solemn all-night vigils (as at the *lectisternia*); everything possible was done to restore the city to divine favor and thus to recover public confidence.

But neither human aid nor the liberal donations of the emperor nor the propitiatory ceremonies offered to the gods could quiet the scandal or dispel the suspicion that the fire had broken out by order [of the emperor]. So, for the purpose of quashing the rumor, Nero substituted as culprits, and punished with exquisite tortures, a group of persons who were [already] hated for their vices, whom the populace called 'Christians'.

I forbear to quote Tacitus's description of the tortures inflicted upon these earliest Roman martyrs. They suffered everything that insane brutality and fanatical superstition were able to devise in that cruel age—the fury of a shelterless mob whose homes had been unaccountably destroyed by fire, which the Christians were now charged with having started; their fury equally inspired by a fanatical hatred born of superstition, for as in all the persecutions the gods were thought to be outraged by the presence of these adherents of a foreign cult; back of all was the diabolical ingenuity of Nero. As the historian concludes, it was evident that the Christians 'fell a sacrifice, not to the public welfare but to the insane cruelty of one man'.

It is as more or less incidental to his narrative that

Tacitus explains how these 'Christians', as they were popularly known, came by that designation:

Auctor nominis eius Christus Tiberio imperante per procuratorem Pontium Pilatum supplicio adfectus erat; repressaque in praesens exitiabilis superstitio rursum erumpebat, non modo per Iudaeam, originem eius mali, sed per urbem etiam, quo cuncta undique atrocia aut pudenda confluunt celebranturque.

The name was derived from 'Christ', who in the reign of Tiberius had been executed by the procurator Pontius Pilate. Repressed thus for the moment, this dangerous superstition presently broke out anew, not only in Judea where it originated but even in the capital—to which everything horrible or shameful finds its way and there enjoys its vogue.

Of course Tacitus is not an ideal historian; he is 'illiberal', 'prejudiced', and 'partisan', as his editors and critics have pointed out. Moreover, he writes perhaps forty-five years after the events in Rome just described, perhaps eighty after those in Judea. Nor does he cite any authority for his explanation of the origin of Christianity: it was probably only the common impression which prevailed in government circles at Rome in the days of Trajan. Yet it is interesting as a purely pagan and secular account, and it is introduced into the narrative at a point not far removed from the date of the earliest surviving written record of the beginnings of Christianity—our Gospel of Mark, likewise written at Rome, and reflecting the horror and the heroism of the first persecution. Distorted as it is, Tacitus's account agrees in general with the New Testament records of Christian beginnings. Galilee is not mentioned; but the death of Jesus and likewise the earliest proclamation of the apostolic message took place in Judea, as Tacitus relates

—and as the gospels and the Book of Acts and the New Testament as a whole affirm and presuppose. Galilee was only a contiguous Jewish territory, still in the days of Tiberius only a dependency, ruled by a tetrarch of its own and not yet incorporated with the Roman province (though the tetrarch, Antipas, had required to be 'confirmed' in his position by the Roman emperor). Tacitus's nouns and verbs are all right, with one exception; it is his adjectives, and his personal bias, that distort the narrative! In this, however, he was not the first offender, nor the last, against the writing of pure history.

There is one further feature in the explanation which deserves to be considered, one which I think has not often been adequately recognized: Tacitus takes it for granted that the movement headed by Christ (*auctor nominis eius Christus*) was already in full swing at the time of his death; the execution of Jesus by Pilate 'repressed it for the moment', but it 'presently broke out anew' and spread not only throughout Judea but even came to Rome.

Tacitus does not use any of the technical language of Christianity—'the Gospel', for example, or 'the Kingdom of God'; he appears not to be aware that 'Christ' is a title rather than a proper noun; and he ignores, or is ignorant of, the story of the resurrection. Evidently his information did not come from a Christian source—though where he obtained it we can only guess. Did it come then from a pagan source, perhaps from a written document, perhaps even from the official report of Pilate to the emperor? Such 'sources' were in existence in the second century: Tertullian (*Apology* 5) takes for granted the existence of such a report—though the documents purporting to give it were recognized by Eusebius, in the fourth century, to be apocryphal, and he gives only a Greek translation of the passage from Tertullian (Eusebius, *Hist. Eccl.* ii.2). The pagan forgeries were clumsy and inexpert affairs, and were completely mixed in their dates (ib., i.9). Still there may have been authentic records at Rome which these pagan apocrypha only pretended to copy.

Whatever the probability as to a written report, it is not difficult to read back, from Tacitus's explanation, to the current Roman version of the events which had taken place in Judea at the end of the twenties, that is around the year 782 A.U.C. That version was certainly more than the story of a handful of disciples following a revered teacher about Palestine until they finally abandoned him at Jerusalem when he fell foul of the religious and civil authorities. On the contrary, by the time of Jesus' death his following formed a widespread popular movement; his followers were ubiquitous and constituted a threat to the peaceful administration of the new province.

This version tallies with certain passages in the gospels, and with some of our other sources, far too completely to be dismissed as mere hypothesis or guesswork. With it tallies, for example, the striking verse peculiar to Luke (23:2)—"Then . . . they made this charge against him: 'Here is a man whom we have found misleading our nation, and forbidding the payment of taxes to the emperor, and claiming to be an anointed king himself'" (Goodspeed).

Now it may be argued that this verse is 'editorial' and simply reflects ch. 20:20, the introduction to the pericope on Tribute to Caesar; though some scholars find in it evidence of a special Passion Narrative which Luke is following at this point, supplementing the Marcan narrative from this additional source. But let us look at ch. 20:20. It also appears to be mainly 'editorial'—a transition from the parable of the Wicked Vineyard Tenants to the pericope about the Tribute: "So they kept watch of him and set some spies who pretended to be honest men to fasten on something that he said, so that they might hand him over to the control and authority of the governor" (Goodspeed). I think this is clearly an editorial transition, introducing the Question of the Tribute.

But, let us ask, need the word 'editorial' connote complete ignorance of the subject in hand, or imply that nothing has been or could be added which was not contained in the sources here being stitched together? Did Luke know nothing about the beginnings of Christianity except what he read in Q, Mark, and L? Or when he supplied additional information was it necessarily of second or third rate quality? We have heard so much about 'stupid' editors, for example those of the apocalypses, that I fear we have unconsciously associated the epithet with editors generally; and have overlooked the fact that all ancient historians—and modern—are editors, revisers, or interpreters of sources; and that when not directly quoting or paraphrasing a specific source they are still 'editing' a body of material which has come to them in various ways, either orally or in writing.

In brief, it is quite unfair to disregard an editor's contribution to the setting of his sources; and though it is true that many of Luke's editorial settings are artificial and merely literary, still when he interrupts a source in order to insert as important a statement as that in ch. 23:2, we must pay careful attention to it. All 'editorial' insertions are not on the same level; each must be judged on its own merits. And I am inclined to think that the charge quoted in ch. 23:2 is something more than a likely speech, written 'in character' and attributed to the 'high priests, temple captains, and elders' (22:52; cf. vv. 2 and 4). It is the kind of charge that would at once demand the attention of a Roman procurator; but more, it is the kind of charge that must probably have been preferred, since Jesus was crucified as 'King of the Jews'. Certainly the first two statements ('misleading our nation, and forbidding the payment of taxes to the emperor') are not 'editorial' in the sense that they were derived solely by inference from the Marcan text or context, which Luke is using at this point: what follows in verses 2c and 3 (the charge of claiming kingship) is certainly Marcan, but it does not follow well after verse 2ab—'King of the Jews' comes in as suddenly and unexpectedly as it does in Mark; and verse 4 seems almost impossible after verse 3: "I cannot find anything criminal about this man" (Goodspeed)— the accusation of his claim to kingship is simply and completely ignored.

In fact, so discordant are verses 2 and 4 with verse 3 that the theory of a special source has much to commend it at this point (and it would support the view which I am advocating); though on other grounds I prefer to look upon the Lucan Passion Narrative as fundamentally Marcan.

Yet on either hypothesis, i.e. whether verses 2, 4, and 5

are 'editorial' or are derived from a specific written source, the standpoint of these added verses is somewhat different from that of Mark (which Luke follows in verse 3). The Marcan view is that Jesus claimed to be 'King of the Jews' —Mark no doubt understood Jesus' reply, σὺ λέγεις, as an affirmation, not a question. But the special Lucan view is that Jesus was charged with being an agitator, an insurrectionist, one who defied law and order and threw the country into turmoil with his teachings, and not only forbade but actually prevented (κωλύοντα³) the payment of tribute to Caesar. As the Maccabees had not only forbidden heathen sacrifices but forcibly prevented them, so Jesus— it was said—had interfered with the collection of the tribute. This was a Judean question, the Roman tribute, not a Galilean one: the taxes in Galilee went to Herod Antipas, not to the emperor—though Herod, like his father before him, knew very well how to maintain himself in the good graces of the emperor.⁴ (It was for presuming upon his friendship with the emperor, spurred by Herodias's ambition, that Antipas finally fell and was banished.)

Thus the charge that Jesus was a disturber of law and order was the chief indictment, according to this Lucan editorial addition; the claim 'to be himself an anointed king' is either incidental or is dismissed by Pilate as ridiculous—as it is likewise by Herod (vs. 11) who 'made light of him and ridiculed him, and . . . put a gorgeous robe on him and sent him back to Pilate'. Perhaps the tetrarch supposed the case too trivial for serious consideration; or, if we accept a recent suggestion by an American scholar,⁵ he may even have thought the best way to win the release

of one of his own Galilean subjects, caught in the toils of
the ecclesiastical metropolis and now in danger of losing his
life at Roman hands, was a bit of festive horse-play. Ridi-
cule might succeed where safe-keeping in prison and even
eventual beheading had proved ineffectual, as with John
the Baptist; and the cases were similar.

Indeed the cases were very similar: as Josephus relates
(*Antiquities,* xviii.5.2 = §§ 116-119), Herod Antipas
"became alarmed lest his persuasive power over the people
might lead to some outbreak (since they seemed to be doing whatever he told them); and so he thought it much
better to act at once and put him to death, before he
started any revolt." John was no solitary prophet; he had
a substantial following, as later indications both in the
New Testament and outside it amply indicate. The interest
of the gospel writers in John the Baptist is concentrated
upon his 'witness to Christ', and so he appears for only a
moment, announces the Coming One, and goes on his
way—though Luke gives in addition an example or two of
his 'social' preaching (3:10-14). But a prophet whose followers were to be found in far-away Ephesus more than
twenty years later, whose movement was still so strong
that a gospel written early in the second century had to
take account of its rivalry to the church, and whose doctrines are thought to be still embedded in the sacred book
of an oriental sect, the Mandeans—such a man must have
had more of a following than Mark, for example, or Q,
would lead us to suspect.

And so it is with Jesus. We are so thoroughly accus-
tomed to think of the beginnings of the church as involving only a handful of men, the eleven, with perhaps a

half-dozen other individuals here and there—e.g. Joseph of Arimathea, or Cleopas—that we overlook the indications in both the gospels and the Book of Acts which show that Jesus' following was very large, and that there really were thousands throughout Galilee and Judea who knew of him and his teaching and were ready to act if he gave the word. It was as the leader of a potential force thought to be threatening revolution that Jesus was put to death and his immediate followers disbanded: this would be not only the Roman view, perhaps more or less formal and official, but it was also, later, the unofficial secular historian's view as well. If Tacitus had expanded his statement he might have said something like this.

The author of the Gospel of Mark of course stresses the claim to kingship, for he is interested supremely in the personal claim of Jesus; it illustrates, if it does not exactly cover, Jesus' claim to be the transcendent Son of Man; though it does not tally at all with the conception of the suffering, dying, and rising Son of Man which Mark has made central to his Gospel (8:31, 9:31, 10:33, 14:21, etc.). And the Fourth Gospel follows Mark in this, as in so much else: the claim to kingship is made the central charge before Pilate—a decided contrast to what precedes, where the teaching of Jesus, and his disciples, formed the subject of inquiry by the high priest (John 18:19, 33, 36, 37, 39; 19:3, 12, 14, 15, 19, 21—the term is bandied about in almost Euripidean dialogue). But John, like Mark, is far more interested in the person of Jesus than in the historical situation; in fact John's interest in history is practically zero; he takes what seems useful for his dramatic or interpretative purpose—and treats even that mainly as background, as the foil against which to set the supreme self-revelation and redeeming work of the Incarnate Word.

The information supplied by Luke in ch. 23:2, 4-5 and in verses 6-12 is the more remarkable in that the author's object, in the Gospel equally as in the Book of Acts, is quite evidently to show that the Christian movement has been from its very beginning one that was not inimical to public law and order. (That Luke included this material must be set down to his credit as a conscientious historian.) Pilate examines Jesus and then says, "I find nothing criminal about this man." Herod Antipas takes no action against him, though Pilate has turned Jesus over to him for trial; Herod merely arrays him in mock-regal splendor and sends him back again. The implication is clear, and valuable for Luke's apology. Nevertheless it is Luke, and Luke alone, who intimates that Jesus' activity, influence, and following could be viewed as a threat to public order. It is Luke, and Luke alone, who explains how the inscription on the cross came to read: "This is the King of the Jews" (23:38). No private, secret claim to Messiahship, in the transcendental 'Son of Man' sense (as in Mark), could explain that to passers-by; only a well known and popular movement, headed by one who was understood to be preaching a message about the Kingdom of God and heralding its arrival, is adequate to give point and significance to the title. Now Luke might of course simply have copied Mark, as Matthew has done, emphasizing Jesus' refusal to answer any of the charges against him—beyond the admission of his claim to kingship. Or he might have elaborated and explained that claim, as John has done, interpreting it in a purely spiritual and other-worldly sense: "My kingdom is not of this world . . . else would my servants fight" (John 18:36). But he adopts neither of these alternatives. Instead he suggests that the ministry of Jesus might very well have been viewed by outsiders, including the Roman procurator, as a threat to the peace of the country: a view that would not be really adequate, and yet was plausible enough if one were not familiar with Jesus' life, character, and teaching. For the 'kingdom' of which Jesus spoke was no purely transcendental, other-worldly realm but a true *Regnum Dei in terra:* God the king of all the earth, reigning in Zion and to the remotest corners of the world. "Thy kingdom come: thy will be done *on earth.*"

If we give due weight to this Lucan evidence we may, I think, obtain a somewhat clearer focus and come to see the beginnings of Christianity in more probable relation to the contemporary world of first-century Palestine. And we may also be in a better position to see how early Christianity evolved and how some of the remains of its earliest beliefs and expectations came to be stranded here and there among the surviving primitive Christian literature: Papias's conception of the earthly kingdom, for example, and the dream of the apocalyptist (Rev. 20) of the thousand years' reign of the saints, and the saying about the twelve thrones (Luke 22:30), and other vestiges of this primitive expectation. To state it briefly, the evidence for the hope of an earthly kingdom is too widespread to be ignored or to be explained away as the result of a later relapse, on the part of the apostolic or sub-apostolic church, from the high, transcendental, purely 'spiritual' and other-worldly teaching of Jesus. That is the necessary explanation, no doubt, if Jesus is viewed as the lonely teacher of a new and esoteric cult of a transcendent, celestial 'Kingdom of Heaven' in which the traditional Jewish eschatology was completely sublimated and 'spiritualized'—not to say evaporated; one who secretly imparted to a chosen few the mysteries of a realm beyond the limitations of time and place, and, above all, shared with them the secret of his own person. There is a suggestion of this view in Mark, it is true; and more than a suggestion, for it belongs to Mark's whole conception of the gospel; but it belongs nevertheless to Mark's 'editorial' treatment of his material (or possibly to a pre-Marcan revision and supplementation of the material) and is not, I believe, found in the most primitive oral tradition. Even as that tradition is represented in Mark it fails to give unanimous support to the 'Son of Man' theology which characterizes the latest level in the Marcan development. For all his criticism of the Law and the Tradition, Jesus was far closer to 'normative' Judaism than to the fantastic and extravagant dreams of an esoteric and quite unrepresentative apocalyptism.

The Gospel of the Kingdom—and this is our thesis—was originally a this-worldly expectation. Jesus expected the Kingdom of God to be realized upon the soil of Palestine, and in his own time. But this does not mean that his hope was non-religious, the elaboration of an economic program or a dream of some kind of mundane utopia. It was supremely religious; but it was not other-worldly, nor was it 'apocalyptic'. The Gospel was a message of *social* redemption, from the start; but as gospel—'good news'—it was a divine message, not a human plan. It stands in line

—at the end of the advancing line—of Old Testament hopes and promises. It envisages the complete and perfect realization of the divine sovereignty here upon earth. As the evangelist Matthew interprets it (for all his high 'apocalyptic' eschatology), "Thy Kingdom come" *means* "Thy will be done on earth as it is in heaven." The Gospel stands in closer relation to the Old Testament than it does to the apocalyptic writings; closer to normal or 'normative' Judaism—even in criticizing it—than to the wild, feverish, bizarre dreams of deluded fanatics; though even these had their points of contact and derivation from the ancestral hope. And from the beginning Jesus' message was addressed to men living within the relationships of ordinary society—villagers, fishermen, farmers, tax-gatherers —not to a select coterie of the spiritually elite, the 'elect' of the apocalyptic circle.

Of course there were various interpretations of Jesus' Gospel, from the beginning. In chief, there were four main types of interpretation of the Kingdom of God: (1) the earthly, to be realized in the future; (2) the celestial, likewise to be realized in the future; (3) the celestial, existing in the present and indeed from all eternity—or at least from the creation of the world—and coming, now or hereafter, in the sense of complete realization; (4) the Kingdom identified with the church, both 'militant' and 'triumphant' and hence combining present and future. It is clear that these views cannot be coeval: a development in thought has taken place within the period during which the New Testament came into existence. The question is, Which is the earliest? Which must be set first, both chronologically and in order of thought, as the one out of which the others grew as a result of the growing experience and the continued reflection of the primitive church? That they were all closely related seems to be clear from the way in which they are woven together in the New Testament, often within the limits of one and the same writing; hence we can hardly assume plurality and distinctness of origin, as some anthropologists assume in accounting for the emergence of the human race! It is our thesis that the basic and fundamental and genuinely historical teaching of Jesus had to do with an earthly kingdom—that is, an earthly realization of the Reign of God—which Jesus expected to see established in Palestine (and everywhere on earth) in his own lifetime. No doubt it was to begin, as the prophets had said, with the 'remnant' of Israel; but it was not to end until, as the prophets had also said, 'The earth shall be full of the knowledge of the Lord, as the waters cover the sea' (Isa. 11:9).

Thus the 'social' Gospel is the original Gospel; that is to say, the Gospel was 'social' in its implications from the outset; the 'social' Gospel really stems from the most primitive and essential element in the whole New Testament account of Jesus' life and teaching. This was the movement of which, as Tacitus says, Christ was the founder; this was the movement that got him into the hands of the Roman authority in Jerusalem; so that, as both Tacitus and the old Roman creed affirm in similar words, 'he suffered under Pontius Pilate'; and this was the movement that, recovering from the blow which had 're-pressed it for the moment', spread with renewed vigor not only throughout Judea, where it originated, but spread even to the capital of the empire.

CHAPTER II

THE TRADITION BEHIND THE GOSPELS

It is now generally recognized that the New Testament reflects a series of stages in the development of early Christianity. The older view which has now been supplanted simply assumed that the Christian revelation took place once for all and was set forth in its final form from the very beginning. One part of the New Testament merely supplemented the rest, one author merely supplied from his inspired thought or recollection what the others had left unsaid—much as in the legend relating the origin of the Apostles' Creed each of the Twelve contributed a clause. Conceivably, on this view, any one of the New Testament writers might have written any one of the New Testament books. But this is not the view of the writers themselves, nor was it that of the majority of scholars in the age of the Church Fathers. The Epistle to Hebrews presupposes a gradual revelation 'in many parts and after divers manners', a principle which presumably is not to be limited to its application to the Old Testament; and the actual contents of the New Testament exhibit a wide range of variety and even of divergence not inconsistent with a central unity of Christian faith and loyalty.[1] Even

controversy was compatible with this central loyalty, as
may be seen from the letters of Paul (e.g. Phil. 1:15-18,
"even so, Christ is proclaimed"), the Book of Acts (cc. 10,
15, etc.), and the Epistles of James, Jude, and Second Peter.
The result, as we now recognize, was that the New Testament produced or reflected a number of different points
of view. There is not one sole and exclusive 'New Testament theology'; there are several different 'theologies'. And
these various 'theologies' are not mere coördinate or com-
plementary sections of one inclusive system; they overlap,
they supplant one another, they are to some extent mutually exclusive. Only a determined and invincible harmonist
will now refuse to recognize the existence of this situation
in the New Testament. The Christian sacred book, unlike
the Koran for example, is not the creation of a single mind,
nor even of a perfectly unanimous community either of
'apostles' or of 'apostolic men' (in Irenaeus's phrase), like
the 'great synagogue' of Jewish tradition. It assumes the
fact of diversity and divergence in human thinking and
experience, from its first page to its last.

And this, we believe, is as it should be. The religion of
the Incarnation takes time seriously, and also human nature. (1) It takes time seriously: the revelation takes place
within the bounds and under the limitations of time and
space. It is no metaphysical idea wandering about in search
of an appropriate vehicle and eventually clothing itself in
a symbolic tale of what might have happened anywhere;
instead, what happened in Galilee and Jerusalem was woven
into the very fabric of history; its events presupposed factors which were concrete and operative in particular times

and places; the revelation could not possibly have taken
the form it did anywhere else in the world or at any other
period in the world's history. Thus the orthodox doctrine
of the Incarnation, based upon the New Testament, was
the very opposite of Docetism with its phantom, semi-
divine Christ; nor could it in any real sense concede the
first principles of Gnosticism with its mythological and
unreal view of history. Christianity on the contrary insisted
upon the hard facts of actual occurrence; the cross was
more than a symbol: it had been made of solid wood tim-
bers and had been set up on a hill outside Jerusalem one
spring morning not many years before; and on it a man
had actually died.

The religion of the Incarnation also (2) takes human
nature seriously. For not only was Christ perfectly human,
and was born, ate, slept, thirsted, walked, talked, grew
weary, faced dangers, was happy, sad, and angry, was
arrested, scourged, spit upon, and suffered the agonies of
crucifixion in full measure; but also the mode and the content of his teaching were human, and his revelation was
made not *sub specie aeternitatis* but *sub specie humanitatis*.
It was no set of oracles he delivered, which some angel
might have conveyed from heaven; they were the sayings,
the stories, the admonitions of one who was completely
and perfectly a man among men and went about Galilee
as a lay-teacher of religion—that is, of the Jewish religion.
Further, the revelation was committed to men 'as they
were able to receive it'; the apostles were not a group of
demi-gods, a college of supermen, on the Christian view,
but actual men—indeed rather ordinary men; not pundits
or avatars but very human persons: Peter, James, John,

Paul, and many others, some of whom were either un-
named or practically unknown but who nevertheless
proved themselves 'ministers of the word'—unimportant
figures in this world, but well known to God. The same
was true of those who responded to their preaching. "Not
many wise . . . not many mighty, not many noble" were
in the Christian calling; but "God chose the foolish . . .
to confound the wise, the weak to confound the strong,"
the base to confound the proud (I Cor. 1:26-29).

So far is Christianity removed from the usual run of the
mythological and imaginary *dramatis personae* of supernaturalism in revelation that most of the figures in its early
history are mere names—as may be seen equally from the
New Testament (e.g. Romans 16), the inscriptions, the
martyrologies, and even the Canon of the Latin Mass. On
the age-old, classical theory, revelations were expected to
come to or through distinguished personages, some king or
high priest, as in Egypt, some philosopher or wise-man
or ascetic, as in India or Greece, through Moses or David
or Solomon or some prophet, as in Israel. But the Christian
leaders were fishermen and farmers and tax-collectors, in
Galilee, and slaves and tradesmen and laborers in the great
Mediterranean cities of the first century.

> Many prophets and kings desired to see
> the things which ye see,
> And saw them not,
> And to hear the things which ye hear,
> And heard them not! (Luke 10:24)

The recipients of the revelation were common people, who
worked for a living and took time from their daily toil

to pass on the good news of the Kingdom. None of them were first-rate writers, none were philosophers, none were professional religious leaders, priests, or scribes. That was the amazing thing: the revelation had been committed to ordinary men and women; the treasure was held in earthen vessels. Christianity took human nature very seriously indeed. One may almost say that God was so sure of the eventual triumph of his truth that he had no care to choose a particular class of men to receive, to safeguard, to defend and hand on the message of eternal wisdom. Even in the gospels Jesus is represented as uttering this prayer:

I thank thee, O Father, Lord of heaven and earth,
    That thou didst hide these things from the wise and under-
        standing
    And didst reveal them unto babes;
Yea, Father, for so it was well-pleasing in thy sight.
                                (Matt. 11:25-26; Luke 10:21)

If then Christianity takes both time and human nature in perfect seriousness, it need not surprise us if the New Testament reflects a gradual growth and development of religion, in successive stages, rather than one unitary impression and response. The New Testament simply could not have been written by one man, or by one group. But this is God's way: he has something to say to everyone, and the mode of his revelation is progressive and partial, not final and comprehensive—though each partial apprehension or insight, on the part of men, adds something to the cumulative result. The full revelation will not be complete till the end of time (cf. John 16:13); its finality is to be seen, not in its present state, nor in that of the New Testament church, but only in the principles of the Gospel, and, back of the Gospel, in the fact, the historic fact, of Christ. For we shall never outdistance him.

I have thought it well to set forth this view in some detail for the reason that, although it is generally accepted in Protestant circles at the present day, we do not always bear it sufficiently in mind as we engage in actual study of the New Testament. Too often we still labor under the needless burden of an unconscious presupposition that every line of the New Testament must somehow be harmonized with every other; or else we assume that, once we have granted the principle of development in the New Testament, then each successive stage must presuppose and build upon all that have gone before. John must be familiar with the Synoptic Gospels, and perhaps with the letters of Paul, and must write with these books before him. Paul's letters must presuppose the record in the Book of Acts and dovetail perfectly with its events and their chronology. Even Mark must keep his theology in line with the apostolic tradition—and, conversely, the apostolic tradition must from the start have included every significant item in the Marcan interpretation, 'Messianic secret' and all. We still incline to read-in the Johannine interpretation, or at least to insert it between the lines of the tradition recorded in the Synoptics; and the later stages of the Synoptic tradition, we assume, may be used to explain the earlier. Q, Mark, and L—if not M—must be in full agreement.[2]

Now there is no doubt that they are, for the most part, in substantial agreement; but their mutual divergences are equally as important as are their agreements in detail—

though, as I say, we tend to emphasize the agreements more than the divergences. I wish we could free ourselves from this more or less unconscious apologetic aim and simply try to see the New Testament as it actually grew, our religion as it actually evolved. It needs no technical 'apologetics'; let it stand forth in the clear light of day, as completely as historical research can reconstruct its earliest development, and it will then commend itself to all intelligent and religiously minded men as something divinely inspired and permanent, a possession for ever to those who can see and will believe.

Thus it is not simply a succession of stages that we observe in the development of the New Testament, but a genuine divergence. Some stages are simply not presupposed by those that follow; some stages are parallel to others, and quite unrelated; some simply diverge, and could not be related (for example the Son of David Messiahship and the belief in the celestial Son of Man); while still other developments ran into dead-ends, and were completely abandoned by the later church: for example the millennial doctrine in the Apocalypse of John (ch. 20), or the obligation to observe the scribal elaboration of Torah in Matthew (ch. 23:2-3), or the limitation of the Christian mission to Jews only (Matt. 10:5-6, 23b). One reason why we are so uncertain upon some points in the teaching of Jesus, and why so many persons are unable to gain a clear, consistent view of his teaching, is that we have tried to combine all the accounts into one uncritical composite.

The same holds true of the popular view of the life of Jesus, and of the mutually contradictory accounts of his career in popular biographies. We have tried to lay one

negative upon another and develop a print that will combine them all; but each negative has a different focus, a
different scale, light, and pose. Theoretically, perhaps a
satisfying composite picture ought to result as the pecu-
liarities of each photograph neutralized those of the others;
only the common elements would be retained and emphasized. But this is not so in fact. What results is often a
caricature, not a resemblance. Of course, let us remind
ourselves, we are not dealing with photographs at all, but
with portraits, or drawings—things not in the least me-
chanical but involving the artist's own skill and insight,
interests, and purposes. Hence a composite view is less than
possible, is in fact quite unlikely to result.

Now it is right here that Form Criticism comes to our
aid. I do not intend to give an account of this latest school
of gospel research: there are already enough books intro-
ductory to the subject. But I would only point out that it
is a perfectly proper method of research; its aim is to recover not only the *form* in which the evangelic tradition
circulated during the oral period (that is really its point
of departure and first task), but also the content of that
tradition. It is no use arguing that a method of 'literary'
research ought not to be used in the solution of a 'historical' problem; for the two go hand in glove, and always
have done so, ever since modern literary and historical
criticism began.

What Form Criticism sets out to accomplish is a further
projection and application of the methods of research beyond and behind the written sources of the gospels. It is
no substitute for Source Criticism, but presupposes it. If

the written (or stereotyped oral) sources of the gospels can now be made out with a fair degree of certainty, perhaps the earlier oral sources, underlying the written, can also be made out. For in the world in which Christianity arose, i.e. in first-century Palestine, oral literature was quite as real and perhaps even more widely current than written literature: witness the legal tradition later embodied in the Mishna and the traditions of the rabbis—that is the anecdotes from their lives. In fact oral literature deserves far more respect than our bookish modern world is inclined to allow it. All the literary peoples of the past and present have known periods when their literatures were oral, not written: witness the Celts, Germans, Gauls, Scandinavians, Russians, Slavs, Hindus, Semites, Spaniards, Egyptians, Romans, Greeks, Chinese.[3] For centuries, history was handed down as legend, before the annals of kings, temple-chronicles, and the archives of states were devised—not to mention the artistic (and sometimes artificial) literary creations of historians. In the East, and especially among the Hebrews, the lives of great men, kings, prophets, religious teachers and leaders, were reported orally and anecdotally, not in written biographies. A biography of Jesus of Nazareth would have been a perfect anomaly in first-century Palestine; if such a book existed, we should know at once that it was a complete fabrication, fictitious and apocryphal, and came from a later age or from another land. Even if it came from another land it would be from a later date. For although the writing of biography was cultivated at Rome, contemporary biography was still practically unknown. Tacitus's life of his father-in-law, Agricola, is almost the first contemporary biography (though Agricola was already dead); while Josephus's autobiography, also written at Rome, was not really a biography at all but an apologia or brief in his own defense.

Back of the gospel sources lie oral traditions. And just as the written sources have been edited by the compilers of our gospels, so likewise the oral sources were 'edited' by those who handed them on. Anyone familiar with the legal traditions of the Mishna and Talmud,[4] or with the Muslim Ḥadith,[5] or with the historical tradition embodied in the earlier books of the Old Testament,[6] or with the Christian *Lives of the Saints*,[7] or with modern criticism of the Homeric epics,[8] will recognize at once that this was perfectly natural and entirely to be expected. Oral literature is not wholly different, in this respect, from written. In fact, oral literature is more amenable to 'editing' than is written: though the remarkable thing is that as a rule it has not been so completely transformed in the process as we might antecedently suppose. Students of primitive literature are aware that proverbs and stories, anecdotes that embody trenchant sayings, parables, and songs, get handed down with a minimum of alteration—often with far less alteration than the materials used by recognized historians, ancient and modern, writing over their own signatures.

More or less the same *kinds* of editing are possible in oral literature as in written. In fact the line between oral tradition and written is not easy to draw, since even after a tradition has been committed to writing it is still possible to revise it from the oral tradition. Some persons will continue to prefer the oral form—Papias was one such early Christian, even as late as the second century—and the written tradition will accordingly be 'corrected' or supplemented from the oral, a later form of the oral sometimes requiring the alteration of what was originally a genuine fair-transcript of the tradition in question. The study of the text, i.e. of the manuscripts of the New Testament, especially of Luke-Acts, makes it clear that oral tradition was still contributing to the formation of the gospels even as late as the latter part of the second century.

In brief, the oral tradition was influential all along the way, from the first written fragments of Jesus' teaching or of anecdotes from his life down to the completed canon of the gospels in the days of Irenaeus, and with desultory contributions, in the way of variant readings, even later still.

Form Criticism is only one further stage in the process of gospel research: first comes Textual Criticism, research of the manuscripts, early quotations, and versions; then Literary Criticism, the study of the finished gospels as they left the hands of their authors; then Source Criticism, by which we endeavor to reconstruct the documents or oral cycles used by the writers; then Form Criticism, the study of the oral tradition as it circulated prior to the writing of any documents, prior even to its incorporation in any cycle or setting, oral or written. But just as the line is not easy to draw between sources and gospels (e.g. between Q and Mark, or between Proto-Luke and Luke), so it is difficult to draw a line between the oral traditions and the earliest sources. Q may have been either a written document or a cycle of stereotyped oral tradition: it would not greatly matter which, in first-century Palestine. One literary form (either oral or written, that is) would have received about the same treatment as the other. This is equally true of L, which many think was even more fluid than Q, not even a unified collection, perhaps, but only the materials gathered in St. Luke's notebook. M certainly had a stereotyped form—so completely stereotyped that, almost like the Mishna, it makes no difference whether this was written down in a document prior to the writing of Matthew's gospel, or first received written form as combined with Mark in the Antiochene gospel (Matthew). M looks like an 'edition' of Q, or of parts of Q, made before Matthew wrote; but whether M itself was written or oral it is impossible to say—impossible, and unimportant.

The parallel case of the growth of the Mishna is illuminating, and is of especial interest in that the two developments were taking place simultaneously; though the Mishna did not receive its present form until sometime about the year 200, while the Gospel of Matthew probably dates from the first or second decade of the second century.[9] There is evidence that small collections of *mishnayoth* were gathered together in the second century and some perhaps even earlier still. Most of these were incorporated in the great Mishna of Rabbi Judah the Prince at the end of the second century, and so lost their separate identity—except for a few blocks of sayings and discussions handed down as *baraitha*.[10] Even so the oral tradition was not exhausted, as the Tosephta or supplement to the Mishna bears witness. The parallel with the growth of the gospels, and particularly with that of the sources of the Gospel of Matthew, is strikingly close.

Since we are dealing with a unified and distinctive oral literature, the (at first) unwritten literature of a cult, and not with the fugitive and adventitious lore of some local hero or shrine, it follows that the principles applying to the criticism of the gospels and their sources may fairly be applied to the oral tradition that preceded the written documents. For example, tendencies observable in the use of the Gospel of Mark by the writers of Matthew and Luke may probably be seen in Mark's own use of the oral tradition with which he worked. Small collections or 'blocks' of material already existed before Mark wrote; these he edited and incorporated in his gospel. Divergences between Matthew's and Luke's rendering of Q (e.g. the Beatitudes and, especially, the Lord's Prayer) may be accounted for, in part at least, by habits or tendencies observable in their use of Mark; though we must reckon with the possibility that similar 'editing' of Q had taken place before Luke or Matthew wrote; and that similar or even somewhat different tendencies (different, that is, from those observable in Matthew and Luke) were at work in the transmission of that collection down separate and divergent channels. And this would be true not only after Q got into written form but even before, while it still circulated as an oral collection of the Lord's sayings.

In the case of such a collection as the Beatitudes, which was no doubt frequently used in teaching and possibly also in worship, and the Lord's Prayer, which was certainly used in common worship, divergent 'uses' in different communities must be reckoned with as a probable explanation of the marked contrast between the Matthean and Lucan versions.

The point to note in this connection is that 'editing' was possible during the oral period, whether or not we can make out in detail the process or its results, or even the principles upon which it was effected; in some places we may be fairly certain of the process, in others we are not so certain. Certainly there were more 'hands' at work here than in the revision of the gospel sources resulting in our written four: though criticism is rightly tending to view the existing gospels less as individual literary productions and more as community possessions. The Gospel of Matthew probably has a 'school' behind it, rather than an individual author; so perhaps has John, though perhaps in less degree—i.e. the book bears more strongly the imprint of an individual author, though the present arrangement of the book requires a considerable discounting of this impression. Mark and Luke are more distinctive, though Mark no doubt relied upon the community tradition and only aimed, as Papias said of him, 'to misrepresent nothing and to leave out nothing'. But the contents of Mark are certainly diversified enough, and represent a collection of material from a considerable variety of sources.[11] It was a complete mistake of late nineteenth-century criticism, as we now recognize, to view Mark as an individual literary creation: the implications of the ecclesiastical tradition of its origin should have prevented that error! But it is equally a mistake to limit the Gospel of Mark to the 'recollections' of one apostle, Peter. There is undoubtedly Petrine material in Mark—but much besides, and from many other sources.

The consequence of this new approach to the gospel tradition, and to the New Testament as a whole,[12] is that we are forced to arrange our materials in genetic relationship, as far as possible, but without trying to knit up everything in one close-meshed scheme of religious thought. The sequence must be genetic, as far as we are able to recover it; but it need not necessarily be chronological. We must recognize the existence not only of variety but also of divergence—in point of view, in manner of presentation, and in the various inferences drawn from or implied by the materials selected for preservation in the gospels. We must recognize that interpretation is not something that began with the history of New Testament exegesis, sometime in the second century, but was an important factor from the very beginning. "These are written in order that ye may believe . . ." "Let him that readeth understand." "Hear what the Spirit saith to the churches." Every saying, parable, anecdote and discourse was loaded with meaning for the group that cherished it, handed it down, and eventually preserved it in written form.

What is required is a clear distinction and classification of the various New Testament interpretations, working backward from the later interpretations (where the ground is more solid) to the earlier, and then cautiously but unhesitatingly advancing upon the oral period. Only so may we hope ever to arrive at a clear and consistent view of the career and the teaching of Jesus and of the origin of the Christian church and its faith. Of course, if we can be content with the blurred and cluttery impression gained by combining all our sources into one, or by picking and choosing here and there, selecting what appeals to us and leaving the rest—as is the fashion of novelists in writing the life of Christ—then we shall save ourselves an immense amount of labor, by dispensing with the slow, patient discipline required for a mastery of the science of historical criticism. But let us not deceive ourselves by thinking that thus we do Christianity any service, or rescue Christ from the hands of adverse critics—as if he required any such service on our part! What we do is only render the whole New Testament and its underlying traditions and convictions suspect. The inference is inevitable that it cannot really face up to historical research, since criticism would soon destroy its fictions and delusions.

I say that this is the natural inference when Christians refuse to submit the New Testament to critical research. No sound bank need hesitate to open its books to the examiners any day they may arrive. The only precaution is to make sure they are qualified examiners, experts, and know what they are about. For criticism, it must be acknowledged, has only been placed under a cloud when applied by men whose real purpose was not so much to get at historical truth as to undermine the foundations of some hated contemporary system of theology or ethics, of ecclesiasticism or of superstition—as they described it. The critic must qualify for his task; he must be willing to spare no pains in getting at the reality of the situation behind the documents and then to follow truth with devoted, selfless loyalty, wherever it may lead.

Chapter III

'THE BEGINNING OF THE GOSPEL':
JOHN THE BAPTIZER

If, as suggested, we undertake to arrange our New Testament materials in the most probable order of genetic relationship, it will appear that the Christian message began with Jesus' announcement of the Kingdom of God. This is also the chronological order of Mark and Matthew. "Now after John was delivered up, Jesus came into Galilee preaching the gospel (of the Kingdom [1]) of God, saying, [The time is fulfilled, and] the Kingdom of God is at hand: repent ye [and believe in the good news]" (Mark 1:14-15 [2]). That is Mark's account of the beginning of Jesus' ministry; and yet the real beginning of the Gospel (1:1) was the baptismal movement and preaching of John (1:4). John's appearance was looked upon by most early Christians as the beginning of the Christian movement (Acts 1:22 ἀρξάμενος ἀπὸ τοῦ βαπτίσματος Ἰωάννου. Cf. Acts 10:37 and Luke 23:5).

Brief as it is, Mark's statement naturally leaves open a number of questions. What is meant by 'delivered up'?— John's death, or his imprisonment? Normally, as used in the New Testament, the verb means 'handed over to the authorities'—not for imprisonment but for execution. In either case, was John's fate the warning that impelled Jesus to leave Judea (or Perea [3]) and begin preaching in Galilee? And had Jesus already been preaching in Judea, perhaps in association with John, for some time before his return to Galilee?—as the Johannine tradition, and perhaps also the Matthean,[4] may be understood to imply (and as Professor Goguel maintains)? Or, on the contrary, is Jesus' work in Galilee the opening of his ministry?

We must, I think, conclude that it is the latter. Prophets do not ordinarily have associates; disciples they sometimes have, but not fellow-prophets on a par with themselves and engaged in the same mission, delivering the same message. Further, Jesus' teaching is too sharply distinct from that of John to make probable their association in preaching. Moreover, the very tradition that represents Jesus as associated with John specifically states that Jesus did not engage in baptism.[5] Further still, the Fourth Gospel, from which the suggestion of this earlier ministry has been derived, does not really picture Jesus as 'associated' with John in the work of preaching or baptizing, but solely as in his company, presumably as one of John's many 'converts' or 'followers', and then as the leader of a similar movement of baptism (though Jesus himself did not baptize, but his disciples, John 4:2). The Fourth Gospel (or one of its main sources, chapters 2-12, the 'book of the seven signs' [6]) definitely supports the Marcan view—in spite of itself—in that it makes the first of Jesus' 'signs' take place in Galilee (2:11) and has the Jerusalem populace look upon Jesus as a Galilean (7:41). In other words, the only tradition we possess on the subject favors the view that Jesus' *ministry* began in Galilee, not in Judea or 'beyond Jordan'. As the Jerusalem (or B) source [7] used in the tenth chapter of Acts affirms, the whole movement associated with Jesus of Nazareth 'began from Galilee after the Baptism which John preached' (Acts 10:37). Even the incidental references bear this implication: for example the slave-girl's words to Peter in the courtyard of the high priest, "You certainly are one of them, for you are a Galilean!" (Mark 14:70, Goodspeed). The words are embedded in the Marcan Passion Narrative, which present-day criticism views as the oldest continuous narrative in the gospels.

The contrary view, that of the Fourth Gospel, viz. that Jesus divided his time between Galilee and Judea, antecedently probable as it may appear, thus has against it the earliest tradition we possess. One would suppose that a prophet, certainly the Prophet Jesus, would address himself to 'all Israel' and not exclusively to the Galileans. And yet, as the late Professor Bacon made clear in his *Gospel of the Hellenists* [8] and in other writings, the Judean ministry described in John is entirely apologetic in aim: it is not to rescue Jesus from despised Galilee, but to claim for Jesus the territory west of Jordan, including both Judea and Samaria, which had been hitherto, and perhaps even at the beginning of the second century still was, the main center of John's following. In the Fourth Gospel the Baptist is only a lay-figure, a foil, a sign pointing to Jesus the 'greater than he'.

If we discount, as upon other grounds we probably must discount, the so-called Synoptic reference to a Jerusalem ministry (Luke 13:34),[9] and if we recognize that the

whole 'Perean Ministry' attributed to the Synoptics by
some modern interpreters is the result of unwarranted
harmonization,[10] then I think we must conclude that the
Marcan representation, supported by the speeches in the
first half of Acts, is true to history, and that Jesus' early
ministry was limited to Galilee. Even if after all there
really was a Judean ministry, as the Passion Narrative
seems to imply, then we can only admit that information
regarding it is almost totally lacking in the New Testament: what the Fourth Gospel provides is material designed
to fill up a recognized lacuna in the earlier tradition, both
oral and written. Turning back to the Synoptic material,
only one or two pericopes are certainly of Judean origin,
e.g. the Question of the Tribute Money, which at the time
was a Judean rather than a Galilean problem. But it is
not improbable that Jesus' final visit to Jerusalem covered
a longer period than the 'holy week' which Mark's arrangement of his material presupposes.

The next question relates to the main subject of Jesus'
message: What was the Kingdom of God, which Jesus
announced? And how was this message related to that of
John? It is a peculiarity of the Gospel of Mark that it
nowhere defines the term. The subject is a mystery, i.e. a
secret revealed to the Twelve (4:11),[11] and yet is referred
to elsewhere as if it were the common property of the
church, i.e. the apostolic message—not to say a subject
which the common people, who were Jesus' first hearers,
readily understood. This apostolic message, viewed as identical with the message of Jesus himself, is simply 'the
gospel' (14:9), which must be preached to all the nations

(13:10)[12]—there is no further reference to the 'mystery'; and when the Twelve are sent out upon a mission, in ch. 6, their ministry is one of exorcism (vs. 7) and healing (vs. 13), and their message is repentance (vs. 12; cf. vs. 11), though Luke explains this by saying that they went out preaching 'the gospel' (Luke 9:6; cf. vs. 2). There is no hint of any specific proclamation of the Kingdom *in this passage of Mark,* let alone any of the intense urgency of the eschatological message which is taken for granted in Matthew's editorial rewriting and expansion of the pericope in his parallel (Matt. 9:35-11:1).

Were Matthew and Luke justified in their assumption that the burden of the disciples' message was the Kingdom of God (Luke 9:2) or, more specifically, the imminence of the Judgment (Matt. 10:7, 15, 23, 32f)? It seems to be probable that Luke, and it is certain that Matthew, had in mind the later apostolic mission, following the death of Jesus, and read its terms and conditions back into the Marcan narrative. If, as also seems probable, the Marcan pericope is based upon or at least echoes a section in Q, then perhaps the later evangelists, who were familiar with that collection, were really justified in both their assumptions, viz.: (1) the mission of the disciples as described in Mark 6:7-13, likewise reflects the later apostolic mission, and was so described even in Q, the source of the later evangelists' amplification; and (2) the message of the Twelve was not only a call to repentance but was also, as the motivation for that call, the proclamation of the Kingdom of God. From the beginning, then, the message of Jesus—and of his apostles—was the Gospel of the Kingdom.

But was the Kingdom of God an eschatological entity, as Matthew certainly assumed and as much of the apostolic preaching took for granted? Or has this emphasis and interpretation been read back into the teaching of Jesus, either by modern exegetes or by the writers of the gospels?

Here is the very crux of interpretation in all New Testament research at the present day. Not only is it of crucial importance for the study and exposition of the New Testament, but it is also of great significance for theology generally, as Barth and his followers—and opponents!—clearly demonstrate. In these tempestuous and terrifying years, since 1914, we seem to be living in a world over which hangs like a suspended sword the threat of inexorable doom. The 'apocalyptic mood' is upon us once more, as repeatedly it has come over one generation and another in the past history of the world, east and west. No wonder that Schweitzer's interpretation of the career and message of Jesus, for all its lack of a sound critical foundation, continues to make a strong appeal to our contemporaries! No wonder if the Barthian theology, which turns topsy-turvy all our inherited nineteenth-century estimates of religious values, seems to many persons the only adequate rendering of the Gospel of Jesus! Our question, though purely historical, has thus a direct bearing upon the preaching and teaching of the church today; for all the more reason, accordingly, we must be careful not to let the modern mood, or a contemporary theology, dictate in advance what our answer must be. We are often warned not to let modern liberalism or modern social idealism color our view of Christian origins;

it is no less needful to beware of the influence of a contemporary theology more conservative in outlook.

We must begin our search for the answer to this question by considering the mission and message of the Baptist. These have been variously interpreted, not only by modern critics but by Church Fathers—and indeed by the New Testament writers themselves. The Fourth Gospel makes John simply the forerunner of Jesus: his last spoken words in the Gospel of John are a plain declaration, "He must increase but I must decrease" (John 3:30). And this is very much the view of the Synoptics as well. John appears like 'Prologue' in one of the old dramas, simply to announce the 'Greater One' who is coming and then to move silently off-stage. Attempts have been made to interpret John as 'the Messenger of the Covenant' (understood to be Elijah)—himself the one his own message had heralded (Mark 9:13); or, on the other hand, to make him a preacher of the Kingdom, sharing Jesus' own message—this is the view of the Gospel of Matthew (3:2; cf. 4:17). Still another view is that John was simply 'a preacher of righteousness', a reformer and champion of morals: John 'came in the way of righteousness' (Matt. 21:32). As Josephus says, he was 'a good man', and died because he roused the apprehension of a tyrannical ruler who suspected him of threatening disturbance and possibly revolt.

Now to some of the Jews it seemed that the destruction of Herod's army [by Aretas, in revenge for the treatment of his daughter, who was Herod's wife] came from God, and justly, as a punishment [not for his treatment of his wife! but] for what he did to John who was called the Baptist; for Herod had put to death this good man who commanded the Jews, after practicing virtue, both in righteousness toward one another and in piety toward God, to come to baptism; for [only] so would the washing be acceptable to him, not as a begging-off [παραιτήσις] for certain sins but as a purification of the body, seeing that the soul was already purified by righteousness. Now when the people had begun to gather—for they came in crowds to hear him—Herod became alarmed lest his persuasive power over the people might lead to some outbreak (since they seemed to be doing whatever he told them); and so he thought it much better to act at once and put him to death, before he started any revolt, rather than regret it later when the revolt had broken out and he [himself] had fallen into difficulties. And so through Herod's suspicion [John] was sent a prisoner to Macherus . . . and there put to death. But to the Jews it appeared that the destruction of Herod's army was an act of divine vengeance, God having determined to punish Herod. (Josephus, *Antiquities* xviii.5.2 = §§ 116-119)

But in spite of all efforts, ancient and modern, to give the Baptist another character and rôle, he seems to have been chiefly a preacher of repentance, stirred by the threatening dangers of the times and inspired, like one of the prophets of old, to proclaim an impending day of judgment when God should bring sinners to account. It is an open question whether or not John's preaching was 'messianic', i.e. whether or not the burden of his message was the announcement of the coming of the Messiah—or even of the messianic kingdom.

The Marcan account (1:7-8) seems to reflect that of Q: note how Matthew and Luke agree in rearranging the introduction and in supplementing the conclusion of Mark's account of John's preaching. As the passage stood in Q it probably read:

I indeed baptize you in water;
But [after me] comes one who is mightier than I,
  Whose sandal's thong I am not worthy to unloose;
He will baptize you [in holy Spirit and] in fire:
  His fan is in his hand,
  And he will thoroughly cleanse his threshing-floor,
  And gather the wheat into his garner;
But the chaff he will burn up with unquenchable fire.
                    (Luke 3:16-17; Matt. 3:11-12)

This can hardly be explained as a passage fabricated for the purpose of asserting the superiority of Christian baptism over Johannine, or the superiority of Jesus (viewed as 'the mighty one') over his forerunner and herald; the passage is doubtless *quoted* for this purpose, but it was quoted simply because, on the Christian interpretation, it was extremely appropriate and relevant. One or two touches may possibly reflect Christian editing—see the bracketed words, above; [13] but the general drift of the passage lies at another angle than that of Christian apologetic, and hence must be viewed as authentic.

Who was the 'one mightier than I' whose coming the Baptizer announced in these threatening words? It is impossible that it could be God himself: no Jew of the first century would have referred to God in such anthropomorphic language, least of all a prophet speaking in his name. Nor can it be the Messiah, the coming king of a free and restored nation, the one 'anointed' by the Lord to reign over his people in peace and prosperity, after conquering their enemies and destroying their oppressors. Not one word of the brief record of John's preaching even hints at the expectation of the King Messiah. The figure

announced by John, and described in the most vivid
imagery, is purely supernatural, and it can be none other
than 'the Messenger of the Covenant' predicted by Malachi
(2:17-3:6), who is to 'appear' for judgment,

> And he shall sit as a refiner and purifier of silver;
> And he shall purify the sons of Levi,
>   And purge them as gold and silver . . .

—in a refiner's furnace so hot that metal flows like wax!
Since he is to be the representative of Yahweh, his judgment will be God's judgment upon the wicked and deceit-
ful:

> And I [i.e. the Lord] will come near to you to judgment;
> And I will be a swift witness
> Against the sorcerers,
> And against the adulterers,
> And against false swearers,
> And against those that oppress the hireling in his wages,
>   The widow, and the fatherless,
> And that turn aside the stranger from his right,
> And fear not me,
>   Saith the Lord of hosts.

So terrible is the approaching judgment that only one
figure is adequate to describe it, *fire*—as also in John's
preaching. This is repeated at the end of the oracle:

> For, behold, the Day cometh, that shall burn as an oven;
> And all the proud, yea, and all that do wickedly, shall be
>   stubble:
> And the Day that cometh shall burn them up,
>   Saith the Lord of hosts.
>
> (Malachi 4:1)

The figure has now changed and become a rustic one, like John's vivid image of the threshing. The motivation is the same in both oracles, 'Malachi's' and John's: it is the threat of swift, inexorable, divine judgment upon the wicked.

At the end of the prophecy some later hand[14] has added two prosaic verses which bend its whole point and close the book with a happy ending:

Behold, I will send you Elijah the prophet *before* the coming of the great and dreadful Day of the Lord:
And he shall turn the heart of the fathers to the children,
And the heart of the children to their fathers,
   Lest I come and smite the land with a curse.

In other words, Elijah is to intervene and save the people, as in the later Samaritan expectation of *Ta-eb,* the Converter,[15] and as in ordinary Jewish folklore and folk-religion to this day. As a result of the confusion thus introduced into Malachi's dire prophecy by the last two verses, many readers came to interpret 'the Messenger of the Covenant' not as the mighty, archangelic, wholly supernatural figure who is to sit in Yahweh's place as the final judge of men, but as the returning prophet Elijah, risen from the dead but still human, and now a milder figure than of yore, whose gentle persuasions and invariable kindliness (as in current Jewish folklore) succeed in effecting repentance and in restoring harmony within the nation—and hence an escape from the divine curse. Others clung to the belief that *both* figures were to appear, first Elijah and then later the heavenly Messenger.

It is this latter view which seems to lie behind the

Christian interpretation of John the Baptist's mission; he was not the Messenger, i.e. the heaven-sent Judge, and certainly he was not 'the Christ'; [16] who else then could he be except *Elias redivivus,* the risen prophet who 'was to come first' (Mark 9:12)? So deeply ingrained is this interpretation in the primitive Christian tradition that it appears not only in the gloss [17] inserted into Mark 1:2 but even in the Q-collection (Matt. 11:10 = Luke 7:27), whence the gloss in Mark may of course have been derived. But the quotation from Malachi has been altered: it is not, "He shall prepare the way before *me*"—as Yahweh's angelic representative—but rather, "He shall prepare *thy* way [before *thee*]", as if the words were addressed to Christ and explicitly referred to John. The change was not easy in Hebrew or Aramaic; but it was perfectly simple in Greek—alter only one letter, let μου become σου, and the whole interpretation of the prophecy is changed. At a time when most quotation was from memory anyway, and when manuscripts were often poorly copied and soon grew faded and worn and partly illegible, such a change could be made in perfectly good faith: a person copying Q or Mark or one of the other Synoptists or some collection of prophetic testimonies would not hesitate to make what he thought the proper correction. A point worth noting, however, is that the change probably took place in Greek, and this perhaps suggests that the interest in John's mission was at least as great among the Hellenists as it was in the Aramaic-speaking circles that handed down the earliest tradition.

It has been suggested that the 'mightier one' of John's prediction was 'the Son of Man', familiar to his hearers

from the vision of Daniel and from the 'Parables' of Enoch,
and destined to play so large a part in the primitive Christian interpretation of Jesus' mission and destiny. But the
close contacts between John's preaching and the oracle
of Malachi are enough to rule out this suggestion. Further,
it is a question just how familiar most Jews of the first
century were with Daniel—where the figure of 'one like a
son of man' is probably only a symbol of resurgent,
triumphant, world-conquering Judaism, anyway.[18] As for
the Parables of Enoch, it seems fairly certain that this
writing (the date of whose final revision is not yet completely settled) was by no means in common circulation,
but was an esoteric work, its readers limited most probably
to an inner circle of apocalyptic enthusiasts. And although
the Book of Enoch—or the circle of ideas which it embodied—was known to the early Christians and the central
figure of its section devoted to Enoch's visions (the Parables) was no doubt influential in the formation of the
primitive Christology, it seems to have been better known
in Galilee than in Judea, where John preached.

The later, that is the Christian, identification of Jesus
with 'the coming one' is reflected even in a passage from Q
(Luke 7:18ff = Matt. 11:2ff), John's inquiry of Jesus,
"Art thou *he that cometh,* or look we for another?"
Quite apart from the questionable presupposition that John
is still living (in prison, Matt. 11:2) at this time, the
words of inquiry may belong only to the 'editorial' setting
or introduction of the pericope (in Q); they would seem
to be quite impossible on John's lips. The 'coming one'
of his message recorded in Mark 1:7 simply could not be
a human person like Jesus. The question is as rhetorical

as that of the Jerusalem Jews in John 1:20; and its whole presupposition is the later *Christian* interpretation of 'the coming one' as the Messiah, and his identification (as Messiah) with Jesus. We must conclude then that the introduction to this pericope *even in* Q (whose wording can be approximately recovered from Matthew and Luke) was 'editorial'. The day has surely passed when Q could be thought infallible, unaffected by any motive of interpretation, and editorially untouched.

John then was a preacher of judgment to come, 'a prophet, like one of the old prophets', and the last of his mighty line. In a day when men still remembered their ancient liberties, but saw with terror and despair the steady advance of an earthly empire destined before long to crush such hopes for ever; when the very air hung heavy with the threat of doom, and the nation was slowly suffocating, first under the tyranny of petty native rulers responsible only to a foreign military representative, the imperial legate in Syria, and then under the direct administration of the emperor's own representatives, many of whom were the typically rapacious, get-rich-quick procurators who battened on the spoils of a helpless people; with foreign troops quartered in the country, and local soldiery, half brigands, plundering their own countrymen; with tax-collectors ubiquitous and insatiable; with poverty everywhere, and hunger periodically stalking the land; with the high priesthood at Jerusalem in the tenacious hands of great land-owning families who cared more for a semblance of public order, the minimum observance of the Law, and their own advantage than they cared for piety or religion; with endless controversy and the bickering of schools and parties taking the place of faith and humility before God; in a generation, to put it briefly, which was sick to death, and had lost the courage and independence of a free people under a king of their own and worshipping a God who rewarded piety with tangible gifts and blessings; among a crushed, downtrodden, and despairing people—suddenly appeared John the son of Zacharias with his flaming message. It was something more than a message of doom—or perhaps something less, and better. For it carried a condition upon which, if men met it, they might hope to escape the coming judgment.

It is easy to see where John got his threat of impending judgment, 'the terrors of the Lord'. It is the psychological concomitant or index of all conquered, despairing, downtrodden people: history is full of it and of the religious reaction it usually produces. Hunger, privation, injustice, tyranny have almost invariably produced the visions of hell, of judgment, and of eventual compensation and the righting of wrongs by some supreme and just power: God, the Judge of all the earth. But this was only a part of John's message. Where did he get the rest of it, the call to repentance, and the symbol of repentance and self-cleansing which he inaugurated, viz. the rite of baptism? Perhaps from current religious practice, within or without Judaism —though it was a century before the custom of proselyte baptism became established in Jewish communities. Perhaps he borrowed it from the Essenes; but the contacts between John and the Essenes seem to have been slight indeed. Perhaps from prophecy: the prediction of a great national lustration before the coming of the New Age, ultimately derived from Isaiah 1:16.[19] But more important was the divine call; as with all the prophets, this came 'from heaven, not from men', as Jesus implied in his answer to the temple authorities (Mark 11:30).

The political situation or its economic consequences taken alone are not enough to account for the appearance of John the Baptizer; it was only one of the conditions favoring his appearance and affecting the form of his message, the course of his career. As Johannes Weiss wrote long ago:

> None of the hypotheses that can be advanced to account for [John's appearance] is as probable as the simple statement of Luke (3:2), "The word of God came upon John". Every historian of religion who sees more in John than empty pretense will take it for granted that only a powerful religious experience could have moved this stalwart, stern, sincere man to speak out the truth to his own people in such severe terms as he used and to threaten them with impending judgment. No one ever arrives at convictions like these by a process of cool rationalization and balancing of probabilities. He was obviously moved by some inner constraint, which his enemies explained as demonic (Luke 7:33). Naturally, the historian cannot explain these antecedents psychologically, but must, if he is to understand the man at all, recognize that elemental religious powers were at work here—powers that are for us, in the last analysis, entirely secret, yet facts: facts with the same reality as the courage of a patriot fighting for his nation's freedom or the tireless energy of a successful statesman. The unyielding firmness of the Baptist, the unconquerable assurance of Jesus—both force us to the conclusion that overpowering religious experiences must have taken place in them. Only so can we account for the inconceivable daring with which they announced the impending destruction of Israel and the end of the world.[20]

Both John and, to some extent, Jesus were what the early Christians described as 'pneumatic', men filled and inspired, indeed possessed, by the divine Spirit. The same was true, in varying measure and degree, of the Old Testament prophets and of all true prophets in the ancient Semitic Near East. "They spoke as they were moved by the holy Spirit," not of their own volition. This involuntary factor was no doubt much more pronounced in John than it was to be in Jesus.

As a preacher of repentance John demanded some token, some expression of the awakened wills and feelings of his followers. And when they plunged themselves beneath the waters of the Jordan and then rose up and came out of the river, surely they must have felt their repentance sealed by a 'remission of sins' which left them somewhat less unworthy to stand before the divine Judge when he appeared. This may not have been a 'sacrament', by later technical definition; but it was surely a rite which brought inner renewal and restoration to countless multitudes. Had it not been such, the practice would have ceased with the death of John; instead, as we know, it survived long after. Josephus is almost certainly wrong: this was more than a lustration 'for the purification of the body'; Josephus must be thinking of the Essenes, or of his teacher Bannus (*Life* ii = § 11), or perhaps of those among his Roman readers who could understand that sort of thing but who would not be likely to make much of 'a baptism of repentance for remission of sins', as the Christian tradition describes John's rite. And yet Josephus does reflect this other view, and goes out of his way to deny it: John was "a good man who commanded the Jews, after practicing virtue, both in righteousness toward one another and in piety toward God, to come to baptism; for [only] so would the washing be acceptable to him, not as a begging-off for certain sins but as a purification of the body, seeing that the soul was already purified by righteousness." This sounds very much like a denial of the Christian view of the meaning of John's rite of baptism.

One thing seems quite certain: John had no message of the Kingdom of God. That was left for Jesus to proclaim.

CHAPTER IV

THE PUBLIC CAREER OF JESUS

It is becoming increasingly evident that the gospels contain only a selection of material for the life of Jesus, and are not themselves biographies; and that the choice of this material was determined partly by the memories of the apostles and others, but chiefly by the needs and interests of the early church. The main body of this tradition was handed down in Palestine, where the Christian communities were no doubt predominantly Jewish; and yet traces of Hellenistic influence are so evident in some parts of it that we must reckon with the probability that although originating in Palestine it was soon transferred to the world outside. Of course Hellenism was to be found in Palestine, and had been found there ever since the beginning of the Greek period in its history; moreover the 'Hellenistic' wing of the Judean church had a very early origin. But the finished gospels certainly did not originate in Palestine: the probability is that Mark was written in Rome, Luke in Achaia or Rome, Matthew in Antioch or its neighborhood, John in Ephesus (or possibly Antioch or even Alexandria); and it is a further probability that the gospels made use of the tradition in the form it had taken in the communities where they arose.

For how long a time this originally Palestinian tradition circulated in Rome, say, or Antioch, or Ephesus, before its incorporation in a gospel or in a gospel-source, it is impossible to say; the tradition—i.e. the available information about Jesus, his words and mighty works, above all his death and resurrection—was no doubt brought there when the church was planted in that city. And a fairly considerable period of time is certainly presupposed by the 'development', i.e. the reformulation and reinterpretation of the old pericopes, reflected in the later gospels. The Gospel of John, the latest of all, presupposes a more extensive theological development than that of the earlier gospels. It also presupposes a peculiar type of tradition, only in part resembling the Synoptic, with one or two pericopes drawn from Mark and rewritten, but in general forming a parallel—or rather divergent—series of incidents, and given a theological interpretation not found in Mark, Luke, or Matthew. And yet John is not unique, except in the degree of its development of theological ideas: for some of these are clearly present, at an elementary stage, in Mark—for example the divine judgment upon the Jews (a *Verstockungsgericht*, as J. Weiss called it), the spiritual blindness of the apostles, the 'mystery' of the Kingdom, and the esoteric character of Jesus' teaching. An astonishing fact about our gospels is that although Jesus was a Galilean Jew, and spoke Aramaic, and the tradition about him was naturally Jewish-Palestinian in origin, our written records are in Greek and reflect that tradition after it had been handed down and developed for some decades in certain Hellenistic Christian communities.

The first task of historical research of the life of Jesus is accordingly a literary-historical one: to work back through the present form of the tradition in our Greek gospels to the underlying tradition as it circulated in the very earliest Christian communities in Palestine, say in the first decade after the Resurrection. This is not to deny that there may possibly have been valuable bits of tradition, i.e. of private recollection, not the common property of the church in the thirties, and not to be brought forward and added to the common stock until later. But we are scarcely warranted in assuming that such traditions were either numerous or extensive, or different in kind or quality from the generally accepted traditions. Apart from John, there is little evidence of an esoteric tradition, a *Geheimlehre;* and the situation in that gospel grows out of the circumstances of its origin: it is not the old tradition but the new interpretation that is esoteric. And so it is in Mark, the earliest Gospel, to the very limited extent that an esoteric element is reflected there: it is not the old tradition but the new interpretation that claims a secret origin and transmission. With very slight exceptions, then, what we have in the old tradition underlying the Synoptic gospels is the common tradition of the gentile churches in the latter half of the first century.

This tradition, we have said, goes back to Palestine. Despite its reformulation to some extent in the Hellenistic communities, its Palestinian origin is obvious. And it appears to go back to two main places of origin, to Galilee and to Jerusalem. There are a few traditions (chiefly found in Luke, i.e. in Luke's special material usually labelled 'L') which relate to places outside Galilee and Jerusalem: some in Judea, one or two in Samaria, in addition to the Marcan anecdotes of the journeys to the north and east. The apostles were Galileans, perhaps with one exception; naturally the narrative and the didactic materials alike are concentrated chiefly in Galilee, that is about the Lake of Galilee, though we know from the other, non-Galilean sources that Jesus had disciples in Judea (Joseph of Arimathea, the two at Emmaus, the group at Bethany, the 'old disciples' in the Book of Acts, for example).

'Q' for the most part is undoubtedly Galilean, not Judean. And it shares with one element in the Gospel of Mark and with the finished Gospel of Matthew a peculiarity which marks it off from 'L', from the editor of the finished Gospel of Luke, and from John, from Paul, and from much of the rest of the New Testament, viz. the 'Son of Man' Christology peculiar to and almost exclusively the possession of these two strands of evangelic tradition. The 'Son of Man' sayings in Mark have been worked into the Marcan tradition at a date prior to the writing of that Gospel; in most cases they can be removed from their present setting; and they reflect a stage, probably an early stage but nevertheless a distinct stage, in the transmission of that tradition. If so, they are undoubtedly Galilean. For the locale of this theology, closely affiliated as it is with the teaching of the Books of Enoch (chiefly with that of the section known as the 'Parables' or Visions in I Enoch) and with other esoteric speculations farther afield, is most probably Galilee: perhaps we should say northern Galilee or southern Syria.

The 'Controversy' sections in Mark, on the other hand, are partly Galilean and partly Judean. The Question about the Tribute Money, for example (Mark 12:13-17), could scarcely have been raised in Galilee, but was a burning issue in Judea now that it was directly under the control of a representative of the Roman emperor.

These characteristics of the tradition of course point definitely in the direction of its reliability: a Galilean source for the teaching of Jesus and most of the incidents of his career, a Judean background for the Passion Narrative and the events leading up to it. An artificial record, say by some Hellenistic romanticist of the second century, could not possibly have provided such self-authenticating details as the 'old' tradition (minus its editorial interpretation) actually gives us.

At the same time, the limitations of the evangelic tradition must be noted. Even a complete outline of the life of Jesus, let alone a full biography, is simply out of the question. (1) The paucity of the available materials and the form and order given them in the gospels alike render such a project impracticable. The arrangement of the gospels is often by subject, and the principle goes back to the underlying sources; and sometimes, especially in Mark and Luke, the order is determined by the method of introducing sources. Luke now follows Mark, now Q, now L, and introduces his sources in 'blocks'. So does Mark himself —he breaks the Controversies into two main sections (2:1-3:6, 11:27-12:34 or possibly 40); his parables are mainly grouped in ch. 4 where he probably relies upon an earlier

collection of them (since his editorial interpretation in
vv. 11-12 is in complete disaccord with the parables
given); the Eschatological Discourse (ch. 13) is wedged
in between the final block of Controversies and the opening of the Passion Narrative—the only place left for it in
the book; all this is evidence that Mark, like the later
evangelists, used written (or stereotyped oral) sources.
Moreover (2) there was not in the lifetime of the apostles
any motive on the part of the church to write what we
should call a biography of Jesus. Our modern interest in
'personality' and in 'personal' history was wholly lacking
and the Jews of that time did not write biographies. This is
a fact to be considered quite apart from the 'eschatological'
outlook of the primitive Palestinian churches, an outlook
that naturally precluded any writing down *by them* of
records for posterity.

The material we possess is accordingly grouped mainly
in Galilee and Judea, i.e. Jerusalem, and the two groups
are connected by a journey, the 'last' journey of Jesus to
Jerusalem. Indeed Mark, our primary source for events in
the life of Jesus (as distinguished from his teachings), is
so largely a Passion Narrative prefaced and introduced by
an account of Jesus' ministry in Galilee that the other
'journeys' of Jesus (through Galilee, to the north, to Decapolis, and around the lake) are relatively insignificant—
mere 'wanderings' during an itinerant ministry of teaching
and healing. In fact it is impossible to trace them on any
map.

As far as we are able to make out from the tradition
recorded in the gospels, Jesus was probably a Judean by

ancestry, if not by birth, but grew to manhood in Nazareth, a village in Galilee. Mark, the earliest Gospel, knows
nothing of his birth in Bethlehem: Nazareth is his πατρίς,
his native place, the town of his fathers (6:1). John, the
latest Gospel, knows nothing of his birth in Bethlehem;
more than that, the scornful references to Nazareth and to
Galilee in that gospel could easily have been answered if
John had known the story in either its Lucan or Matthean
form (see especially John 1:46, 7:41-42). A simple statement would have sufficed: "True, he lived in Nazareth of
Galilee, but he was born in Bethlehem." On the other hand
the wholly divergent Nativity Narratives in Luke and
Matthew agree in affirming Jesus' birth in Bethlehem,
though in little else; while from other authors comes the
testimony that Jesus was 'of the seed of David' (Rom.
1:3), and 'sprung from Judah' (Heb. 7:14; cf. Rev. 5:5).
The tradition of his Judean descent is therefore not only
older than the story of the Nativity, but older than the
Gospel of Mark which makes Nazareth his native town.

If we were faced with this problem in an area of 'secular'
history, or in the Old Testament, we should not hesitate to
suggest the obvious solution: Jesus was a Judean by descent, though a Galilean by birth and upbringing. Perhaps
that is the solution to be preferred here—though to many
it will not seem to go far enough. The location of his
birth was transferred to Bethlehem in order to conform
with Old Testament prophecy, as interpreted in the early
Palestinian church. Whereupon it became necessary to
explain how he was taken to Galilee in infancy and grew
up there—two entirely different explanations being offered
by the Nativity Narratives in Matthew and Luke. There

were Judean families in Galilee, and had been ever since the Maccabean war of independence had made possible the return of Jews to their homes in that district. There were Judean families even in the Diaspora, outside Palestine; and there were other old families as well—Saul of Tarsus was descended from the family of Saul the Benjaminite. That Jesus was a full-blooded Jew is unquestioned, save by such writers as H. S. Chamberlain who would rewrite all history, ancient and modern, in the interest of their theory of 'Aryan' supremacy.

Nazareth, where Jesus grew to manhood, was a village in Lower Galilee, not far from the busy towns of Capernaum (on the Lake of Galilee), Sepphoris (just north of Nazareth, in the foothills of Lower Galilee), and Tiberias (on the west shore of the lake). So far as we know, he never visited either Sepphoris or Tiberias; they were seats of government, and both were probably largely pagan towns. The royal bank was located at Sepphoris. But Capernaum became the headquarters of his ministry.

About the year 28 or 29, as we have seen, the nation was aroused by the appearance of a fiery prophet of repentance, John 'the Baptizer', whose message drew hearers from all quarters, and who bade them seal their 'renewal' by immersing themselves in the waters of the Jordan river. The heart of his message appears to have been the approaching advent of 'the Messenger of the Covenant', not the Messiah but a wholly supernatural figure, the representative of Israel's God, the angel of the Lord, who should sit in judgment and pass sentence upon the wicked and separate the wheat from the chaff. The coming of this Messenger from God is described in language similar to that of the apocalyptic writings; but the core of John's 'prophecy' is drawn directly from the Book of Malachi—the book of 'My Messenger'—not from any of the apocalypses. The only possible escape from the severity of the impending judgment was the old prophetic way of repentance, to be symbolized and sealed now by the self-administered rite of baptism in the Jordan. Whether or not he headed or 'founded' a sect is not certain; fasting and set forms of prayer as well as baptism appear to characterize his following in the period after his death. There are later traces of a Johannine sect, e.g. in the Book of Acts (18:25, 19:3); but whether or not this sect grew into that of the later Mandeans is another question.

Like many another, Jesus went to hear John and was baptized or rather baptized himself; Matthew's conception of the scene (Matt. 3:13-15) reflects later Christian usage. For a time Jesus may have been in some way associated with John, though this is unlikely; as we have already observed, his own independent ministry began only after John had been either thrown in prison or—surely soon afterwards—put to death. As Josephus relates, Herod Antipas, the tetrarch of Galilee and Perea, feared John's growing popularity and so shut him up at Macherus, a desolate 'castle' east of the Dead Sea, where he was put to death. Mark's story of John's martyrdom (6:17-29), following his rebuke of Herod's unlawful marriage, does not contradict the statement of Josephus and may be accepted as an added detail explaining Herod's antagonism—though the tale has the features of later legend and a *motif* completely different from that of the account in Josephus.

What was Jesus' own attitude as he approached the

baptism of John? Devout imagination has sought the answer to this question, almost from the beginning of Christian history, and has very naturally found an answer by reading into the record the presuppositions required to account for Jesus' later career. Luke's account of the incident from Jesus' boyhood (Luke 2:41-51) with its precious saying, "Did you not know that I must be at my Father's house?" has been taken as an indication of a dawning 'messianic consciousness'; but it is only the expression of the normal piety of a Jewish child, brought up in a wholesome religious atmosphere. Matthew's account of John's reluctance to baptize Jesus (Matt. 3:13-15) and Jesus' reply, "It is right for us to do everything that God requires," is the solution of a later difficulty, viz. how could Jesus have undergone a 'baptism of repentance for remission of sins'? And yet the words may express what was really in Jesus' mind: whatever God has shown to be his will, including the baptism of John, which was 'from heaven, not from men', must be mandatory upon the conscience of every Israelite.

Beyond this the records say nothing; the gospels are not biographies. What we must suppose then is that Jesus was a devout and faithful 'son of the Torah' and lived the Jewish life in loyalty and devotion; he was no dissenter, no lax and careless and non-observant Jew, no 'am ha-aretz' in the later opprobrious sense—though he lived among that group and ministered to them. He was a faithful, devout Jew, with a mind nurtured upon the divine revelation in the Old Testament, 'the Law, the Prophets, and the Psalms': though loyalty to Judaism did not yet involve the full rigor of the later legalism or all the multitudinous minutiae of the scribes. Yet this tells us little. For deep at the heart of his religious life lay the motive of complete obedience to the will of God, complete response to the revelation of God, and the peace which passes understanding and comes only from perfect union with God. This much we must assume; but it is not in the record —rather it is the inference we must draw from the life, the character and teaching of Jesus viewed as a whole. How much else there is which the record does not tell us! (John 20:30-31; 21:25).

The hour of Jesus' baptism is identified by Mark with an inner experience which he and the other evangelists interpret messianically. It was the Baptism rather than the Resurrection, or the Transfiguration, or Peter's Confession —let alone his birth, or a state of divine preëxistence— which seemed to the evangelist Mark the appropriate beginning of Jesus' Messiahship. (He knows nothing of any 'Messianic consciousness'; both the abstract term and also the idea, partly theological, partly psychological, which it expresses are wholly modern, and never entered the mind of a first century Christian.) The other Synoptists follow Mark in this identification, though it conflicts with their representation of his divine conception, birth, and early life. The Fourth Gospel disregards the significance Mark has given it, and transforms the incident into an experience of John the Baptist (1:32, "I have beheld . . ."); the preëxistent Logos had no temporal beginning of Messiahship, either of office or of 'consciousness'.

What the experience of baptism actually meant to Jesus is not easily made out: Mark's interpretation fits only too well into his plan to demonstrate that Jesus was the Mes-

siah, not from the day of his Resurrection but throughout
his whole earthly ministry. Some kind of prophetic vocation or call is indispensable at the outset of Jesus' career.
Surely "no man taketh this office unto himself except he
be called of God"—this would be the unanimous and inevitable feeling of every first-century Jew, indeed of every
ancient Hebrew, Jew, or Arab. For to Judaism and to the
Semitic world generally there was no such category as
'mere prophet' (another modernism!): the prophet was
the highest conceivable human manifestation or emissary
of the Most High. As late as Maimonides (*Mishneh Torah*
i.7.6), Moses himself, exalted to the highest possible human
category short of divinity, is 'The Prophet' of the Eternal.
Next to God himself speaking in audible tones, the prophet
was his spokesman, apostle, messenger, and the interpreter
of his will. This claim was in fact made for John the
Baptist: "Of those born of women, no greater than John
has ever appeared." "And yet," replied Jesus, "he that is
least in the Kingdom of God is greater than John" (Matt.
11:11, Luke 7:28).[1] Certainly Jesus would not accept
such a place for himself in the divine plan, that is as
God's prophet, without a clear and unmistakable call.

But whether or not Mark is right in dating Jesus' Messiahship or messianic vocation from this hour, is another
question. As already noted, it tallies only too completely
with Mark's purpose to show that Jesus was already Messiah during his earthly life (and not from the day of his
Resurrection, as the older tradition took for granted; see
for example Rom. 1:4). Some modern scholars hold that
Jesus' 'Messianic consciousness' grew gradually; some even
trace its beginnings in his youth, following analogies found

in other areas of religious experience. Others hold that if this consciousness ever emerged in Jesus it must have come later.

Now Mark's conception of the 'Messianic secret', of the Messiah in disguise, is altogether too patently artificial. The Jesus of the parables, of the healings, the preacher of the good tidings of the Kingdom of God, is no Messiah traveling about incognito. If anything is certain, it is that Jesus had no wish, either then or ever, to be the king of Israel, the political head of his people: and that is what 'Messiah' always meant for Judaism, apart from the vagaries of the apocalyptists and the transformation of the concept effected by the early Christians.

It is much too simple a solution to say, "Jesus was conscious of a call to be the Messiah, but he transformed the conception—chiefly along the lines of the Danielic 'Son of Man' concept, now elaborated in the Apocalypse of Enoch, and by combining with it the idea of the Suffering Servant of the Lord as set forth by the Second Isaiah."

For any human being to identify himself with the 'Son of Man' of the visions of Enoch, taken literally and without reinterpretation, could suggest little else than an unsound mind—certainly not the supreme and unquestioned sanity of the Man of Galilee; yet of any 'reinterpretation' or 'spiritualization' of the concept there is not one hint in the gospels. Furthermore, what would come of such reinterpretation? The figure is wholly impersonal; his function is in no sense essential to redemption; he is after all only the symbolic representative of 'the Lord of Spirits' at the Last Judgment. And what can be made, by any method of reinterpretation, of his coming 'on the clouds of heaven'?

In the second place, it is historically improbable that Jesus identified himself with the Suffering Servant and consciously set about fulfilling the scripture, 'faithfully carrying out the last symbolic detail'.[2] Such arbitrary fulfilment of prophecy was too artificial a procedure for such a person as Jesus, and for a Jew would moreover have been simply presumptuous, indeed blasphemous—as blasphemous as his journey to Jerusalem would have been, had he gone there, as Schweitzer maintains, 'to force the hand of God'. That is not the Jesus of the gospels! But as categories under which the early church looked back and interpreted the saving Act of God which Jesus' whole life, death, and resurrection had really expressed, both the Son of Man conception and that of the Suffering Servant were filled with a new and deep meaning.

How then did the church come to view Jesus as the Messiah, and to identify him both with the Son of Man and with the Suffering Servant? The historical answer is clear from the whole New Testament: It was his victory over death, his resurrection and glorification as Messiah, that led to this identification. But such a conviction was impossible without a prior confidence in him which went beyond devotion to a beloved teacher. He was a teacher, but something more; a prophet, but more than a prophet, a *ḥasid*, a saint, a godly teacher who also healed the sick and worked other miracles, but something more than a saint. He was in some real sense the Bringer or Bearer of the Kingdom, the one 'in whom all God's promises were yea' and received—or were to receive—their fulfilment. This was the basis of their faith in him; and at such a time, and under the circumstances, what could be more natural than to use the terms that lay near at hand to express that growing faith?

But what of Jesus himself? Into the luminous depths of the mystery of that wholly unique personality we may not peer with prying, curious eyes. But at least this we can say: Here was one whose mind was wholly set upon God, whose will was completely one with the will of God, who 'spake as never man spake' and thought as never man thought because the very center of his being was fixed upon the Eternal. The rest of us, the countless children of Adam, can only murmur, even in moments of highest religious exaltation,

> The current of my being sets to thee.

But here was one whose whole being flowed *with* God, not merely toward Him; flowed *from* God, rather than simply toward Him. We cannot define him; the miracle of his person is something ineffable and beyond all definition, even all description. He was unique. He was divine. And that is something which the strange titles of ancient apocalyptic messianism not only fail to convey but positively misrepresent; something which even such a magnificent conception as that of the Suffering Servant does not begin adequately to set forth. It is not that he is less than Messiah or Suffering Servant; instead he is vastly, incomparably more. His uniqueness does not lie in his 'fulfilment' of earlier prophecy—though among other things the primitive church recognized that he had done that: let alone a conscious and purposeful carrying out of 'each symbolic detail'. It lies rather in a quality of life, that 'spirit of life which is in Christ Jesus' (Rom. 8:2).

This, rather than miracles, fulfilments of prophecy, 'claims' to various titles messianic or other—this *spirit of Jesus* is the ground of the church's faith in him, as Paul made clear in the greatest of his Christological utterances, the hymn in Philippians 2:6-11. For Christian faith, it is this 'quality' or 'spirit' which is the most real thing in the universe and the completest possible manifestation of God.

The fact is, as Gressmann [3] and others have made clear, 'the Messiah' was only *one* form of the eschatological expectation then prevalent in various circles in the Near East. Another was 'the Son of Man', originally, as in the Book of Daniel, a mere symbol for the anticipated triumph of the Jews in the days of the Maccabees; then literalized, as in the Book of Enoch, as the transcendent and indeed preëxistent divine being present with God from the creation of the world and destined to be the coming supernatural Judge of the living and the dead and of the spirit-world as well. This conception, which as we observed had an influence upon the earliest tradition of Jesus' sayings, probably owed not a little to the prevalent conception of the Primal Man found in areas entirely outside that of Jewish apocalyptic and therefore presumably anterior to it.[4] Paul's conception of the second man, who is 'from heaven' (I Cor. 15:47), owes not a little to this circle of ideas; Johannes Weiss—in his comment on this passage— even held that 'the Man from heaven' was Paul's reference to 'the Son of Man'. At any rate the conception presumably originated before Paul's conversion, as a part of the tradition he 'received' (I Cor. 15:3). Paul's gospel, as he insists, was not derived from Jerusalem; that it contained apocalyptic elements is both obvious and so claimed by himself. If we could reconstruct the religious beliefs and concepts of the Christians in Damascus before Paul's arrival, or even those in Antioch before he came there; or if we could discover the content of Paul's own 'visions and revelations', at Damascus and 'in Arabia' and elsewhere, we might then be able to recover the antecedents of his Christology—which are certainly somewhat different from those of Q and Mark, not to mention the other gospel sources. And where are we to look for a more likely point of contact between the age-old Iranian, Mesopotamian, and generally Levantine speculations upon the 'Anthropos' or 'Primal Man' than in Damascus or 'Arabia' at the time of Paul's sojourn there?

The Messiah was only one figure among many; and the selection and combination of two or more of these figures was the work of various circles within early Palestinian or Syrian Christianity—a process which had already taken place and was still to continue among other groups, Jewish, semi-Jewish, and non-Jewish, down into the second century and even later. The distinctive feature of the *Christian* synthesis of apocalyptic figures and symbols was that for all Christians, apocalyptists and non-apocalyptists, the Coming One was identified with Jesus the Lord who had lived and died and risen again and was still to come 'in glory'.

Only on some such hypothesis as this can we relieve the historical Jesus of intolerable contradictions and an unsupportable burden of unreality. He was certainly no mad fanatic, no deluded pretender to a celestial and really mythical title, no claimant to a throne which did not exist, no prophet of a coming judgment to be carried out by a heavenly figure seated on the clouds with whom he identified himself—which judgment never took place, never could take place. That idea was the cherished hope of one circle within the early church—but of only one. There were other Christians whose outlook was non-apocalyptic, non-eschatological, and to them we owe the preservation and transmission of the greater part of the tradition of his words and deeds. The tradition has been influenced by the 'Son of Man' dogma; but it has not been completely transformed. If there are passages in the gospels that show clear affiliation with the Book of Enoch, there are plenty of others that betray no such influence or affiliation. And it is not difficult to determine which are the more unmodified and authentic.

It is probably due to the influence of the document (or cycle of sayings and parables) known as 'Q' that Mark locates the Temptation at the outset of Jesus' ministry, though he omits the details—which are best preserved in the order of Matthew. From Matthew it is evident that the story is a piece of apocalyptic symbolism, entirely 'literary' in conception though doubtless originally oral in form, an account of the Ordeal of the Messiah, and appropriately set at the beginning of the Sayings Collection. From what ultimate source it was derived no one can say. That it is from some other source than the main body of Q appears to be evident not only from its style and structure and its use of the Old Testament (in the Greek version), but from its Christological title: Jesus is addressed by the tempter, "If thou art *the Son of God.*"

This reflects a different Christology from that centering in the Son of Man concept. As a portrait rather than a record of Jesus it is important: for it divines the attitude which, knowing him as his followers did, he must have taken when confronted by the various alternatives of current messianism. It is a picture of Jesus as he must have reacted to the Satanic suggestions of personal aggression and aggrandizement, compromise with secular power, histrionic display and self-manifestation: that is, supposing such motives ever appealed to him at all. The two basic *motifs* are Jesus' identification of himself with the Messiah (i.e. 'Son of God'—the term is peculiar to this section, in Q) and the popular nationalistic idea of the messianic office. The story is simply the dramatic collision of these two opposing forces, ending in Jesus' victory over the tempter.

Returning to Galilee after the imprisonment or death of John, Jesus began his work of teaching and preaching in Capernaum. The family carpentry in Nazareth was forsaken: only some time later, and very briefly, was he ever to visit Nazareth again. His ministry, outwardly viewed, was one of reading and exposition in the synagogue, frequent public teaching of the crowds and of smaller groups in private, the healing of the sick and the exorcising of demons. In a country where modern medicine was unknown, and even Greek medicine little practiced, and where popular belief ascribed all sorts of ailments to demonic possession, with all the malicious suggestions, social and individual, that this involved, it was little wonder that a prophet or *ḥasid* should be confronted with constant appeals to exorcise evil spirits. This was so much the case that Jesus even found it difficult to pursue his main task of teaching without diversion and distraction. And it brought with it the opposition of the scribes and Pharisees, who, not denying his cures, sought to parry the inference men drew as to Jesus' supernatural authority by ascribing them to collusion with 'Beelzebul', a local 'chief of devils'. Yet he never abandoned his ministry of healing, and he even sent out his apostles on a mission similar to his own; for he saw in the success of his exorcisms no personal triumph but the evidence of the arrival of the promised Kingdom: "If I by the finger of God cast out demons, then is the Kingdom of God come upon you" (Luke 11:20).

Teaching, healing, the calling of disciples, their mission to share in his work and prepare for his own visits to new places, then a period of retirement beyond the lake, a longer journey to the north (perhaps occasioned by the suspicious interest of Herod Antipas, following the death of John), controversies with the scribes and Pharisees, the incident of the visit to Nazareth, and the growing hope on the part of the disciples that he himself, not John, might be the 'prophet and more than a prophet', the destined fulfiller of Israel's hopes—such are the incidents that fill up the busy days and months of his ministry in Galilee, as far as we can make it out from the scanty records before us.

Outwardly viewed, as a series of events, there is no progress, little order. The arrangement of the tradition recorded in Mark (upon which all the other evangelists are in large measure dependent for such order as they observe) is determined partly by subject, partly by the collocation of related material which had already taken place in the sources, oral or written. It is just the situation we find in the tradition of anecdotes from the lives of prophets, rabbis, and saints—Jewish and Mohammedan as well as Christian—save that neither Jews nor Arabs ever wrote gospels. We have no right to expect chronological sequence, biographical order: not only Mark but all the evangelists wrote οὐ μέντοι τάξει, as Papias (in Eusebius, *Hist. Eccl.* iii.39) reported 'the Elder' as saying of the earliest of them: 'by no means in strict order'. True, Mark has an order; (1) he leads up steadily to the Passion Narrative, and (2) he presents Jesus as acknowledged to be the Messiah, both by human beings (Peter) and by superhuman (the demons, and the Voice from heaven), long before the Passion. But, as many scholars now recognize, this 'pragmatism' of his is forced upon the tradition. The confession of Peter is a dramatic narrative of the apostle's triumphant faith in a Messiah who was not only traveling incognito, but was now even in exile—outside Jewish territory, in 'the neighborhood of Caesarea Philippi'. And Peter's faith in Jesus' Messiahship is guaranteed by the succeeding experience of the chosen three on the Mount of Transfiguration. This is either an account of a resurrection appearance which has been antedated and shifted back into the Galilean ministry,[5] or it is the account of some ecstatic experience born of exalted faith, told and retold in terms similar to the accounts of the resurrection and hence influenced by the latter. Whichever it be, it has quite obviously been made a part of the Marcan scheme of proofs, i.e. of Jesus' heavenly Messiahship even during the months of his earthly ministry; and hence it ought not to be used as a biographical datum, especially since no use is made of it later in the story.

As Passover approaches, Jesus turns southward, perhaps (as Mark suggests) avoiding a direct route through Galilee and detouring by way of Decapolis and thence journeying southward through Perea and down the Jordan Valley. Such a route avoided undue publicity, and thus also escaped the attention of Antipas and his 'Herodians'.[6] Even so, Jesus was recognized by followers and friends, and was welcomed by the common people who always 'heard him gladly'. Apparently, as the Fourth Gospel assumes, there was a widespread popular belief—or at least a suspicion and a hope—that he was the coming one, i.e. the messianic 'king', 'who should redeem Israel'—a view which some of his own disciples no doubt shared, and which led to the popular demonstration and acclamation at the descent of the Mount of Olives, the incident known as 'the Triumphal Entry'. How far Jesus accepted this outburst of enthusiasm on the part of his disciples and followers and the crowd of pilgrims we can only surmise. The Marcan story of his own preparations for the demonstration— whether due to the author, or, more likely, to the form of the tradition that lay before him—is quite out of keeping with Jesus' own conception of the Kingdom as non-political, and contradicts that view of him expressed elsewhere in the gospels—e.g. in the 'portrait' of him given in the Q-narrative of the Temptation; or in Matthew's quotation, 'a bruised reed he shall not break, nor quench the burning flax' (12:20); or in John's version of his reply

to Pilate, 'My kingdom is not of this world' (18:36). If
he entered the city in this fashion, it was as a prophet (as
Matthew specifically says, 21:11), not as messianic king;
and the demonstration is one more of the prophetic 'signs'
or symbolic acts, like those of the Old Testament prophets,
designed to protest in the name of God and of his revelation (through Zechariah) against the militant, aggressive,
materialistic nationalism whose violence and fanaticism
already presaged, forty years in advance, the destruction of
the temple and the holy city.[7]

The immediate climax of the 'triumphal entry' was the
so-called cleansing of the temple. Appealing to the inspired
words of the prophet of old, 'My house shall be called a
house of prayer for all nations' (Isa. 56:7), but adding,
from another prophet, 'Ye have made it a den of thieves'
(Jer. 7:11), and with complete disregard for all the con-
ventions and conveniences that really meant compromise,
desecration and profanation, he advanced upon the money-
changers and the dealers in doves, and, armed only with a
whip of cords (so John 2:15), drove them out. "And he
permitted no one to carry a vessel through the temple"
(Mark 11:16), thus further protesting against its casual
profanation. That in this action he had the support of the
enthusiastic crowd which had accompanied him into the
city, we cannot doubt. Even the children shared the popular exultation (Matt. 21:15). But his triumph was short-
lived: the traders would be back again on the morrow!
He had no intention of establishing himself in Jerusalem
by force of arms—the most his disciples could muster was
'two swords', or, more likely, two long knives, such as the

peasants used for cutting brush. And so he withdrew, late that afternoon, and went out to Bethany.

The following day he returned to the temple; and there, day by day, he taught the people, debated with the scribes, slipped out of the verbal traps which were set for him one after another by scribes and priests, Pharisees and Sadducees. The question of the tribute he adroitly parried by insisting that what belonged to Caesar should be paid to him, what belonged to God must be paid to him likewise. This answer was more than an evasion of a difficulty; it set forth in substance his whole protest against the materialism and fanaticism of his generation. To the question regarding the source of his authority he replied with another question. "Tell me: The baptism of John, was it from heaven (i.e. by divine authorization) or from men? Answer that, and I will tell you by what authority I act (cf. Mark 11:29-30)." This also was more than a clever retort. His Socratic replies opened up new vistas, and led men—if they would only look—to see beyond the immediate present situation to the far horizons that environed Jesus' whole ministry, outlook, and teaching.

But the climax of his dramatic entry into the city, followed by his attack upon the settled routine of the national sanctuary, soon brought the counter-climax of opposition to him. At last the hierarchy had him in their power—or they soon would have, if they could only lay hands upon him, 'quietly, and before the feast actually began, lest there should be a riot among the people' (Mark 14:2 Codex Bezae). He had dared to carry his disturbances to the very temple, the heart of Jewish conservatism and propriety. What the scribes had said of him in Galilee was only too true! Unless he were shut up or put out of the way, the insurrection they feared would surely take place; and with that the modicum of self-rule still left them by the Romans would undoubtedly be withdrawn. And so the Council—or more likely a junta of its leading members, the group about the high priest—determined to make away with him before it was too late. There could be no tolerance for one who threatened the temple, who announced in so many words its coming destruction, and who doubtless intended another assault upon it as soon as the city was filled with pilgrims and when, among them, his own followers had gathered in force.

At this point came the offer of Judas to deliver him into their hands—not to betray his 'Messianic' claims or self-consciousness; for of this there is no word in the record, nor was any such 'betrayal' used as testimony at the trial. What Judas offered was to lead a band to Jesus' retreat at night and turn him over to them. This offer they accepted. Jesus' fate was sealed, as far as human eye could see.

Following their supper in an upper room—the 'Last Supper', not the Passover meal [8]—Jesus and his companions went out to the Garden of Gethsemane: though how they passed the city-gate, which was closed at sundown, is not said. Here Judas came with his band of temple police and slaves, and they seized Jesus and led him to the high priest's house. At the arrest, the disciples made a momentary attempt at defence; but seeing it to be useless, especially since Jesus himself made no resistance, 'they all forsook him and fled.'

In the high priest's house was gathered a small group, probably not the whole Sanhedrin, and an effort was made

to force Jesus to convict himself by some admission or
other that could be used as a formal charge before the
Sanhedrin in the morning—and before Pilate. But Jesus
again foiled their efforts, this time by complete silence.
To the accusation that he threatened to destroy the temple
he made no reply, and the testimony of each witness apparently cancelled out that of the others, so that no use
could be made of the charge. Just what further procedure
was followed is not clear; none of his disciples was present;
the story is related from hearsay, and from inference and
imagination. As it is told in the two later Synoptics,[9] the
question was finally asked by the high priest whether or
not he claimed to be the Messiah, and at last Jesus spoke:
"So you say—$\sigma\grave{v}$ $\epsilon\hat{i}\pi\alpha\varsigma$: that is how you conceive him—
but instead of an earthly Messiah, a king in Jerusalem, you
shall see the Son of Man seated at the right hand of the
heavenly Power, and coming with the clouds of heaven."
(Both Matthew and Luke avoid Mark's round affirmation,
$\epsilon\gamma\acute{\omega}$ $\epsilon\grave{\iota}\mu\iota$: for Jesus is really *not* King Messiah, the Royal
Pretender in disguise, but the heavenly Son of Man.)

Whatever Jesus' precise reply, and however it was understood, his words were construed as an affirmation of Messiahship, and it was as an insurrectionist, a lawless, dis-
turbing *roi prétendant* that Jesus was condemned by the
Sanhedrin in the morning and handed over to Pilate.
Stoning was the penalty for blasphemy;[10] but here was a
charge that could lead to more certain death, and without
the risk of popular disturbance or riot. The Roman governor would take full responsibility; moreover, the Council
would earn his thanks for handing over a disturber, thus
proving their zealous concern for law and order. It was a

clever plan and, assuming that the Galilean would continue his policy of silence, one that would doubtless succeed. It succeeded. Jesus refused to answer the charge
against him—his cryptic reply to Pilate's question, "Are
you the king of the Jews?" may be itself a question, as
Hort suggested: "Would you say so—σὺ λέγεις?" or even
an imperative, "You say!" i.e. "What would you say?"
When Pilate, as Luke relates, endeavored to pass on the
responsibility to Herod, perhaps hoping that he would
free a Galilean, one of his own subjects, the tetrarch sent
him back arrayed in a tattered mockery of royal robes.
Even so, according to Mark and the later gospels, Pilate
again attempted to set him at liberty, and proposed his
release as an act of benevolence in honor of the festival.
But the fanatical priests would have none of it; and so
Jesus was handed over to be scourged and crucified. Over
his cross was set the diabolical lie of the priests: "This is
the king of the Jews."

It is often said that the inscription on the cross proves—
or at least confirms—the statement that Jesus claimed
to be Messiah, and was put to death on account of his
claim, which the Jewish authorities rejected. Does it follow then that every claimant to kingship during the
troubled days following the death of Herod was a *messianic* claimant? Josephus names some of these (*Antiquities*
xvii. 10 = §§ 250-298): Judas, Simon, Athronges, and
implies that there were many others.

Judea was full of robbers; and whenever the seditious found
a leader they proclaimed him a 'king' and set forth to do mis-

chief to the public. They did some small damage in minor ways to the Romans; but the murders they committed among their own people continued for a long time (§ 285).

On the contrary, these 'kings' were only leaders of bands of freebooters and guerrilla warriors, and made no claim, so far as we know or suspect, to be Messiah. Their wild careers, ending when Varus crucified two thousand of the seditionists (§ 295), illustrate the passage in John 6:15, where the Galilean multitude came and tried by force to make Jesus 'a king'. They also show how Pilate could be convinced that Jesus was another leader of the multitude, in a class with Bar Abbas 'who during the insurrection had committed murder' (Mark 15:7), and deserving to be crucified as one more 'king' of a band of lawless and violent 'robbers'. 'Robbers' is the standing designation in Josephus for these discontented and insurgent groups of would-be revolutionists.

The story of the Crucifixion, though it is motivated here and there, like the Passion Narrative as a whole, by Old Testament references understood as having found their 'fulfilment' in the death of Christ, can still be made out in its probable historical sequence. It is the story of many another in that dark, fanatical age. Thousands died at the hands of Rome, nailed or tied to crosses, and perishing of thirst—e.g. the two thousand crucified by Varus. What is distinctive about the Christian story is the character, the spirit, the attitude and bearing of the Central Figure in the tragedy. When, as the Fourth Gospel relates, the three on Calvary were ordered to be despatched, after some hours of agony, lest their bodies remain exposed over

Sabbath, Jesus was already dead. Why he died so soon, when men often lingered for days, is not told; the later Christian interpretation, involving psychological or 'spiritual' factors, is probably right. His death was hastened, not by physical exhaustion but by mental anguish.

As Mark and the other Synoptists tell the story, he died within a few hours, and according to Mark and Matthew his last words were from the twenty-second Psalm: "My God, my God, why hast thou forsaken me." Luke substitutes an appropriate saying from another Psalm; but the addition is perhaps his own, however appropriate. John substitutes still another utterance, one with a deep theological, mystical import, "It is finished."

The burial of Jesus was temporary, in a near-by grave, hewn out of rock, belonging to an otherwise unknown disciple, Joseph of Arimathea. The women who had followed him and his disciples from Galilee prepared spices, and when the Sabbath was over they came intending to prepare his body for permanent entombment. But, as Mark relates, their mission was never fulfilled—for the body of Jesus no longer lay in its cool, rock-hewn grave. He had risen from death, and was already, according to one tradition, en route to Galilee, there to keep rendezvous with his disciples; according to the Lucan tradition, he appeared to them in Jerusalem, and in the neighborhood, and 'by many infallible proofs' showed himself alive after his passion. The very earliest accounts of all represent Jesus as rising from death *as Messiah* and appearing in vision to his apostles. As Johannes Weiss and others have pointed out, the stories of the physical resurrection and of the empty tomb are much later than those of the visionary appearances.[11]—But this is not the last chapter in the life of Jesus; instead, it is the first chapter in the long history of his Church.

According to St. Paul, the Resurrection of Christ is the cardinal point in the religion which bears his name, more important, more central and fundamental than even his death. For in it was summed up, and through it was mediated, not only Christ's own victory over death but the new life which was his gift to all his followers. "Christ being raised from the dead dieth no more; death no more hath dominion over him" (Rom. 6:9). And if we are buried with Christ, in the likeness of his death in the flesh, we shall be raised with him unto newness of life—a life of victory over sin, over the flesh, over that death which is the penalty of all sin in the flesh. Paul, like John and many other early Christian writers, is more interested in the permanent religious significance of the Resurrection of Jesus than in its details as a historical event; and yet he fully recognizes the importance of the evidence for it, as a historical event. As a matter of simple fact, the evidence for the resurrection of Jesus, a 'spiritual' resurrection, in a 'spiritual body', transformed and incorruptible and perceivable only in 'vision', is actually more in quantity than the evidence for his death! And the consentient testimony of the earliest as of the latest witnesses is that Jesus rose from death, not as a man restored somehow to life, like Lazarus or the youth at Nain, but as the glorified, triumphant Christ. "Thus it behoved the Christ to suffer, and [so] to enter into his glory" (Luke 24:26).

But it is not as the King Messiah of the Jews, the *roi*

prétendant now at last declared to be the rightful occupant of an earthly throne; it is the heavenly Lord of the Church who rises from death. That is the testimony of the earliest faith and preaching of the apostles. And if we doubt that Jesus ever was, or ever intended to be, the Jewish Messiah, that is not to deny his divinity, or—let us say it fully—his deity. We still repeat the rich, profound, ancient phrases of the Nicene Creed with no hesitation but with fullness of confidence; for they are still the only words really adequate to our conception of him: 'God from God, Light from Light, very God from very God, begotten, not made'. 'Light from Light', for he is in truth, and by no poetic metaphor, the very light by which we see light, the master-light of all our seeing; and never more truly than now; and ever more truly as the years pass by and the long centuries slip away to join that distant past which separates him, historically, from us. For it is not simply as a figure in history that we adore him: he is the living Lord, ever present, ever with his church, still at work in the world, 'conquering and to conquer', and with ages on before still waiting to acknowledge his influence and to receive the gift of life from him. It is, in fact, not simply the historical Jesus taken alone—if that were possible—but the Spiritual Christ revealed in him, who is 'God manifest in the flesh' and the hope of the ends of the earth. It is still 'the law of the Spirit of life in Christ Jesus' that makes us 'free from the law of sin and of death' (Rom. 8:2).

It must of course be remembered that the gospels are later than St. Paul—the very earliest of them about twenty years after Paul had begun writing his epistles; and that for Paul what was significant in Jesus was not his message, or his career, or his miracles, but his divine-human character and his triumph over death (cf. Phil. 2:1-11). He was a Messiah, but in a new and much more wonderful sense: not Messiah of the Jews (though his thought of Christ had begun with that idea, apparently), but 'the Man from heaven' [12] manifest upon earth and redeeming men from the power of sin and its consequent death. For Paul, 'Christ' is no longer a title but a personal name. There were no national or local limitations in Paul's message about Christ; and it may seem strange that any biographical knowledge (i.e. tradition) of Jesus' life had survived out in the Graeco-Roman world where the earliest written Gospel was produced.

For all this, Paul clearly presupposed a knowledge of the life and teaching of Jesus.[13] But it was only the Palestinian tradition, largely unaffected by Paul's teaching, that preserved the human portrait of Jesus and something of an account of his life. (1) And this account, this body of tradition, has to be examined as a Semitic product, not Hellenistic, not Western, not Pauline. (2) At the same time it must be recognized that 'the great church', already coming into existence in the Pauline mission field, had apparently begun to dispense in some measure with the miracles of Christ (save for the supreme miracle of his resurrection) and had already dispensed more or less completely with the nationalistic Missiahship and Kingdom. (There were still Jewish prerogatives, as Paul insists in Romans, chs. 3 and 9-11; but they are being indefinitely postponed, and are ultimately to be harmonized with the cosmic victory of Christ only in a somewhat obscure and unspecified way.) This is a situation that deserves the most careful pondering.

In his recent inaugural lecture at Cambridge, Professor Dodd has made a strong plea for the interpretation of the New Testament *as a whole*.[14] It is the deposit of the spiritual life of a new movement in human history during its earliest, formative period: this deposit was at first oral, then written, though its 'historical' literature was written considerably later than the epistles of Paul. Every document contained in the New Testament requires for its full interpretation the whole life of this new movement; but not every document reflects its total life.

The gospel literature, for example, does not reflect the whole of early Christianity but only one phase of it: mainly the Jewish, Palestinian phase. Its interests are somewhat different from those of Hellenistic, Gentile, non-Palestinian Christianity—even though Mark and Luke and probably John were written by Gentiles. The gospel traditions, arriving at the written stage somewhat late in the first century, are still redolent of the soil of Palestine and still reflect the interests of the early Jewish Christian communities.

(It is easy to overdraw this contrast. Luke's Gospel is certainly 'Hellenistic' enough in interests and aim; so is Mark—not to mention John. And there is obviously a 'Hellenistic' factor in the composition of Matthew. And yet the Synoptic *sources* are clearly Palestinian and Jewish Christian. What purely 'Hellenistic' motives could do in the way of producing gospels is evident from the New Testament apocrypha: they either merely repeat, sometimes with absurd misconception, the statement of the canonical gospels or else launch out upon the uncharted deep of simple, unguided fantasy.)

The gospels represent a development parallel to the Pauline, Gentile type of Christianity; and yet relatively to that other type they are somewhat belated not only in time but also in growth of thought. Paul's conception of Christ, for example—as far as we can reconstruct its beginnings—apparently began at a further stage of development than even Matthew, the latest of the Synoptic gospels, succeeded in reaching; while his conception is quite different from both Mark's (the disguised Son of Man) and from Luke's (the true King of Israel). And John's Gospel represents still another stage. Or, rather, it represents not so much a stage as a wholly different line of development, post-Pauline and influenced by Paul (to a degree that the Synoptics are not), and yet independent, flourishing in a world of ideas quite distinct from that of the Christian synagogues or Nazarene assemblies in Palestine.

Thus the early Christian movement pushed forward into history like an army in several divisions, not wholly parallel or concurrent in their advance, one moving more rapidly and more easily than another, one halting rather than steadily advancing, another even retreating after a swift initial advance (e.g. the Apocalypse of John). No neat chart showing the chronological sequence of the New Testament writings will at the same time make clear its inner course of evolution. That took place variously, and obviously not without cross-references and influences and reactions (e.g. Paul and the churches in Judea).

Hence the Synoptic gospels, to be rightly understood, must be viewed in relation to the conservative Christian tradition of Palestine [15] upon which they are based, and the types of Christianity developed there, without reference to Paul and the Gentile churches. And although it is a mistake to suppose that either Pauline Christianity or Gentile Christianity generally apart from Paul was wholly unhistorical in origin or interests, it is clear that the Palestinian traditions, when finally set forth in Greek gospels, do not fit at once into the framework of ideas of Gentile Christianity.

And yet it is Gentile Christianity rather than Jewish, if a choice must be made, which is *our* type of Christianity: or, rather, it is Gentile Christianity as derived from Jewish but at an earlier stage than that represented in the gospels (Paul, e.g., was converted probably sometime between the years 35 and 39 A.D.), and then pursuing its own course of development more or less independently of the Palestinian tradition. This is our type of Christianity: that of the ancient Greek Church, that of Western Christendom, Catholic and Protestant, to this day. Early Eastern Christianity, i.e. Jewish or Palestinian, where not stamped out in the fourth or fifth centuries or in the eighth, went its own and very different way and finally died out. Ebionism was simply a form of Palestinian Christianity in its decadence; so was Docetism; and so were some of the old Eastern heresies, in so far as they were not the by-products of Greek Catholicism or of reaction against it in the second century and later (e.g. Gnosticism). But *our* Christianity has been from the first non-traditional, metaphysical (at least in tendency), in a sense super-historical, *übergeschichtlich*.

CHAPTER V

THE BACKGROUND OF JESUS' MESSAGE

It may be well to summarize the argument up to this point: The earliest reference to Christianity in secular history is the brief account Tacitus offers in explanation of the persecution of the Christians which broke out after the burning of Rome in the year 64. From this sketchy and hearsay account one may gather that Roman officialdom looked upon Christianity as a movement headed by a person named Christ, a movement which not only began but was in full momentum before his death, and was only checked temporarily by that catastrophe. Further, it was a movement which had political implications, and had accordingly been dealt with by the Roman procurator, Pontius Pilate. Eventually—but it is not said when—it had come to Rome, along with the other subversive movements that flowed inevitably into the capital. With this all too brief and prejudicial account tallies in part at least one strand in the gospel narrative, chiefly Luke's account of the charges brought against Jesus at his trial before Pilate. From these slight but important indications it may be inferred that the movement led by Jesus was of wider influence than the main body of the evangelic tradition, in its present form, would lead us to assume. True, we hear of 'the multitudes' again and again in the gospels; and the Galilean 'multitude' was no small potential force, as we learn from Josephus's account of the Jewish War. Nevertheless, although the Gospel of John preserves the tradition that at one time the people 'would have taken Jesus by force and made him king' (6:15), still the general representation of the gospels is a very different one. There Jesus is accompanied by a handful of disciples; of these only three or four are really important; and his contacts with 'the multitude' are limited almost exclusively to healing and teaching—'the political relations of Christ's ministry', to use Stephen Liberty's phrase,[1] are almost obliterated in the gospels as they now stand. We may suspect, then, that the Gospel of the Kingdom really had a social or possibly even a political reference from the start: we should expect to find that it was a Kingdom to be established here upon earth, not a transcendent state of bliss in the after-world. That was our first point.

In Chapter II we considered the oral tradition of Jesus' life and teaching as it is reflected in the gospels. There is variety—even variety of interpretation—in the New Testament: even variety of interpretation in the gospels! And this is as it should be, considering the social and non-literary origin of the tradition. The solution of the problem which this involves is not to be sought by the old method of harmonization; instead, we must examine each strand of tradition separately, and even each pericope, without reference (at first) to the interpretations found in other strands lying side by side with it in the gospels. For this is the way of oral tradition, and each transmitter of tradition is an interpreter of tradition. Back of the final editors of the gospels were other interpreters, who each added his contribution as the accounts of Jesus' ministry and teaching grew—at first the simple narratives, sayings, parables, as used in the preaching of the primitive community, then the collected gospel sources, finally the completed gospels as we now have them. If interpretation was thus present from the beginning, the course of the recovery of Jesus' life and teaching—the historian's task!—can only be one of similar interpretation, viz. the recognition and isolation of this interpretative element in the tradition. Some parts of the tradition, touches added here and there to the narratives or even to the parables and sayings, and also the completely variant form given some of the sayings, reflect perfectly the exegesis of the early church. This was prior to the evangelists, and was quite as important in its results as was their attempt to coordinate and interpret the ministry and message of Jesus as a whole. Indeed, their interpretation depended in no small degree upon this earlier interpretation made in the course of oral transmission. Hence the gospel materials must be analyzed and arranged in genetic relationship, as a body of church-tradition (that is, the tradition of various *groups*). This arrangement may or may not be chronological; we cannot tell. But it is the only possible way, if we are to make progress as historical students dealing with a very involved and complicated body of historical tradition. Chapter II was accordingly an interlude on the subject of method, and an explanation of the method adopted.

Chapter III opened up an approach to the historical background of Jesus' ministry by a reconsideration of

John the Baptist. John's message appears not to have been a proclamation of the coming of the Messiah—that is later interpretation—but rather a flaming message of impending doom, of the coming judgment which was to be held by the supernatural Messenger of the Covenant, God's own representative. The only recourse for those confronted with this judgment was the way of repentance, to be sealed and symbolized by a self-administered baptism of the penitent in the river Jordan. Though 'the beginning of the gospel', i.e. of the movement headed by Jesus, dated from the appearance of John, that prophet himself was not really a member of the New Kingdom: "he that is least in the Kingdom is greater than John." The contrasts between John's message and that of Jesus are more striking than the similarities. But it was a true interpretation, nevertheless, which saw in John's work the preliminary preparation for the message and ministry of Jesus. John had plowed the hard fields and broken up the stony clods; over the fields thus prepared Jesus had sowed the seed of the word, and had seen the new harvest spring up—a very different harvest than John anticipated, but one for which nevertheless he had helped prepare.

In Chapter IV we discussed the career of Jesus as a whole, as far as it can now be made out upon the basis of historical material in the gospels. But it must not be forgotten that the gospels are neither histories nor biographies, but works written to preserve the traditions of different groups, to interpret those traditions, to set them in a proper light for inquirers from outside, to arrange them for purposes of teaching and indoctrination. And they are fragmentary. No life of Jesus was prepared for inclusion in some first-century 'Universal Cyclopedia of Biography'. No historian of first rank gave even a chapter to the life of Jesus. The gospels are documents of faith, written 'from faith, unto faith': "These are written that ye may believe" (John 20:31).

And yet it is possible to make out with some assurance the probable course of events—particularly in the Passion Narrative, the account of Jesus' last two days in Jerusalem. The historian's task is not altogether hopeless. We are dealing with a body of oral tradition that has crystallized into brief collections, and has then been worked into longer books. But to evaluate it properly it must still be translated back into its oral form—the separate pericopes that circulated in the early church. The longest consecutive narrative we have, at this oral stage, is the Passion Narrative—less than two chapters of Mark, but probably a continuous narrative almost from the very beginning.

We also considered once more the importance of interpretation in the oral period, and the probability that two or three types of Christianity, rather than one, were current even in the early Palestinian church. Hazarding a guess, it would seem that the Christianity which used the current messianic terminology of Judaism and of the Old Testament, i.e. the nationalistic messianism whose favorite term was 'Christ' or 'Son of God', belonged more properly in the south, in Judea and Jerusalem; while the Christianity which adopted and adapted the apocalyptic scheme reflected in Enoch, with its favorite term, 'Son of Man', belonged in the north, in Galilee or Syria. That there were at least two centers of early Christianity in Palestine seems indisputable, following the researches of Bacon, Lohmeyer, Lightfoot, and others.[2]

The reason why this was not recognized earlier is probably due to our dependence upon the Lucan history. Luke-Acts was written upon the assumption that the church spread from Jerusalem; here, rather than in Galilee, the appearances of the Risen Lord had taken place; here the apostles were commissioned to evangelize the world, 'beginning from Jerusalem', and embracing Judea, Samaria, and eventually 'the uttermost part of the earth' in their advance (Acts 1:3-8). The Book of Acts recounts the triumphant progress of the Gospel from Jerusalem, the capital of Judaism, to Rome, the capital of the empire—for which perhaps Luke felt the same pride that many another felt in the Augustan age and later, believing that the capital of the empire was destined to be the capital of the entire world (cf. Luke 2:1). As a result of Luke's schematic arrangement, and of his ignoring of the Galilean Christians—though his traditions do not entirely ignore them (cf. Acts 9:31, 21:3-7)—we have been led to assume that primitive Christianity was practically non-existent in Galilee.[3]

But it is contrary to all expectation to suppose that the movement headed by Jesus should have come to nothing in his native state, and succeeded only by transferring its headquarters to Jerusalem. Moreover much of the gospel tradition, as we have noted, points to Galilee not only for its place of origin but also for its transmission.

Now we do not say that the 'Son of Man' Christology was unknown outside Galilee. Stephen's dying words in Acts (7:56), the vision that opens the Apocalypse of John

(1:13), the words of the martyr James, from Hegesippus (see Eusebius, *Hist. Eccl.* ii. 23. 13)—these alone are enough to prove the contrary, not to mention the finished gospels of Mark, Luke, and Matthew, and the repeated reference even in the Gospel of John (including the extraordinary one in 12:34, "Who is this 'Son of Man'?"). But the center from which that theology was disseminated and so got into the gospel tradition, and the place where it most strongly affected the tradition as it was being handed on, was, we believe, somewhere in 'Galilee of the Gentiles'—a place in close and constant contact with the religious hopes and expectations of the surrounding world, and likewise a center of the apocalyptic 'school' or group which produced the 'books' of Enoch—now collected in our 'First Enoch'. There can be little question that the Enochic literature was produced by a group which cherished, preserved, edited, compiled, and handed on the various parts of this weird writing. That the literature was still in process of compilation and editing even in Christian times and by Christian editors is evident from many of the interpolations and from later imitations. Indeed, we may justly suspect that in its present form I Enoch should be dated somewhat later than Charles and Beer have assumed.

There is one more preliminary consideration, and in the present chapter we shall deal with the general background of Jesus' message. It is the background not only of Jesus but also of John, and of the generation that heard them; it is also the background of the whole early Christian movement. It is therefore indispensable for an understanding of what Jesus meant by 'the Kingdom of God', and of what his hearers understood him to mean. Some of them, like Judas and even others of his close disciples, appear to have misunderstood him completely.

For two generations now, the Mediterranean world had been at peace—comparative peace, the only kind it has ever known. It was a new era, men thought. Something approaching Virgilian religious enthusiasm for the empire is reflected in Paul's and in Luke's references to it. It was nothing less than a heaven-sent boon. For it came like the dawn of a day of perfect calm after weeks of raging tempests. In fact ever since the middle of the fourth century before Christ the Mediterranean world had been in almost constant turmoil. In 338 Philip of Macedon had won the battle of Chaeronea and spread his sovereignty over the whole of Greece. Two years later his son Alexander succeeded him, and in 334 he set out to do with the Persian Empire what Philip had done with Greece. The next eleven years record one of the most epical advances of political power in all human history. The Persian Empire fell like a house of cards before young Alexander of Macedon and his skilful generals with their superb fighting units, the Greek phalanxes. Soon after his death, Alexander's vast empire of conquest was divided, mainly into the four kingdoms whose history fills out the tale of the Near East until the coming of Rome.

But in the west also, during these years, there was movement; between 343 and 272 B.C. the Romans conquered middle and southern Italy, the Latins, the Samnites, and crossing the Adriatic to Greece conquered Pyrrhus of Epirus. The barbarian Celts from the north were repelled, and were shunted along the Balkan peninsula until they finally settled down, around the year 272, in north central Asia Minor, where they were to be known later to New Testament readers as the Γαλάται, 'the Galatians'. By now the Romans were gazing across the narrow seas to the south and confronting a foe with whom they were to battle to the death: the first Punic war ended in 241, the second in 201, the third in 146. In the end, Carthage was destroyed, even as the senator Cato had pronounced its doom, and Rome was now free to turn its attention eastward. It had, in fact, already done so, intervening in the affairs of the eastern kingdoms as opportunity arose, and every time advancing a step further the military or commercial gains or claims of one power and of one only, Rome. In the year 190,[4] for example, at the end of the first decade of peace following the second Punic war, the Romans defeated Antiochus III at Magnesia in western Asia Minor; the Seleucid kingdom recoiled upon itself, staggering and trembling from the blow. Twenty-two years later the Roman legate Popillius Laenas drew a line with his staff about the son, Antiochus IV, as he was about to enter Alexandria, and bade him consider the step before taking it. Nation after nation in the Near East was now falling before the continued military, diplomatic, and commercial strategy of the aggressive westerners. By 200 the Romans had a strong foothold in Egypt; in 146 Macedonia itself was to become a province, in the same year, Greece; in 133, the kingdom of Pergamum, in northwestern Asia Minor, was to fall. The row of dominoes had begun toppling, and almost every decade saw new additions of territory, population, and resources to the republican empire of Rome.

Hemmed in now on the south, in the north and west, Antiochus IV determined to unify and consolidate his kingdom and prepare for the coming storm. The Jews, who occupied his southern frontier, were to be Hellenized by force, and the unity of the Seleucid state and its religion and customs thereby guaranteed. Incidentally, the rich treasures of the temple in Jerusalem would be useful in providing the sinews of war. This decision was reached on Antiochus's way back from the Egyptian frontier, in the year 168; the immediate consequence was the Maccabean revolt. It was a successful revolt, thanks partly to the courage and military skill of the Maccabees; partly to the heroic sacrifices of the Jews, who were prepared to die rather than give up their ancestral religion; partly to the internal weakness of the Seleucid kingdom and the continual intrigues, plots, and counter-plots that marked its decline. Three years after the desecration of the temple, i.e. in the year 165, worship was restored once more; two years later complete religious freedom was granted the Jews—though a Syrian garrison held the Akra on the eastern hill in Jerusalem for over two decades more. Complete independence was gained in 142, and Simon the Maccabee was proclaimed (in 141) to be 'high-priest, general, and ethnarch of the Jews', with the right to hand on the dynasty in succession to his heirs (I Macc. 14:35-49). But the eastward advance of Rome, as we have observed, was already well under way, and the Maccabean dynasty lasted for only eighty years. By 63 B.C. the whole of Syria was in Roman hands, and Egypt was soon to become a province.

The old political problem emerged once more—this time as a problem for Rome to solve. Politically speaking, the Jewish state stood squarely in its way. The tiny principality made up of Judea, Samaria, Idumea and Galilee straddled the great arterial highway of trade and communication which joined Syria and Egypt, and in fact linked Rome and the west with the Far East. Geographically Palestine was part of the land-bridge between the three continents. The coastal trade with India, for example, crossed southern Palestine by caravan from Alexandria or from Gaza; while the trade by land with Damascus, Palmyra, Edessa, Mesopotamia, the lower Tigris-Euphrates Valley, Persia and the East naturally made use of the roads running north, east, and south through Palestine. More than all this, the military situation demanded a united eastern frontier. It was impossible to leave an open sector in the broad front which swung like the arc of a shield from Egypt to Armenia, from the Red Sea to the Black. Already the Parthians were astir, and menacing. Perhaps no one in Palestine realized the necessity of a unified frontier; but the shrewd senators and consuls in Rome realized it, and so did their officers in the field—Pompey, for example, who turned his attention to Palestine the moment Syria became a province and its affairs were somewhat settled.

The last of the Maccabees were quarreling over the succession, Aristobulus II and his brother Hyrcanus II. For five years the quarrel had continued, and in the year 64 an embassy was sent to Pompey requesting him to settle the strife. He came at once to Jerusalem with a body of troops. The party of Aristobulus was besieged and defeated; Aristobulus was taken as a captive to Rome; his brother Hyrcanus was made high priest, and Judea became a vassal state! The gates had been opened to the Romans, and they were never again to be closed until the Roman was within the walls and securely in possession of the city. Along the fringing and more open frontier of Samaria and Galilee, farther north, the old Hellenistic towns were restored, reorganized, and attached directly to the Province of Syria—the Ten Towns or 'Decapolis' of the gospels. In Judea a kind of local procurator or commissioner was appointed, to oversee the collection of taxes. This was Antipater the Idumean, father of the Herod who a generation later (in the year 40) was made *rex socius*, allied king.

In the meantime the second Roman civil war had broken out, involving now the whole Near East. Crassus had fallen at Carrhae in 53, fighting the Parthians; the other two remaining members of the first triumvirate, Caesar and Pompey, were locked in a death-struggle, ending with Caesar's victory at Pharsalus in 48. Through all this turmoil, Antipater had managed to maintain himself in power, and fell only at the hand of an assassin the year after Caesar's death (43 B.C.). The year 40, when Herod was made king by decree of the Roman senate, saw the advance of the Parthians in Syria, and their incursion even into Palestine. In 32 began the fourth civil war, Octavian against Antony and Cleopatra, ending two years later with the deaths of the latter and the incorporation of Egypt into the empire. The shrewd policies of the house of Antipater, the adroit shifting of loyalty, the clever sensing of imponderables, the unfailing devotion while devotion was

commendable, the swift change to a new master when that
master was in a position to demand service—all this adroit
political acumen and dexterity inherited from his father
was practiced by Herod with the utmost skill.

His rewards were apparent at once. The year after the
battle of Actium and the triumph of Octavian, Herod's
territory was increased by the emperor's gift of seven important cities: Gadara, Hippos, Samaria, Gaza, Anthedon,
Joppa, and Strato's Tower—which a decade later he re-
built in honor of Caesar and renamed Caesarea. Hyrcanus,
since 47 the high priest and 'ethnarch' of the Jews, was
executed and thus put out of Herod's way. With the
beginning of the reign of Augustus, in 30 B.C.,[5] Herod
accordingly settled down to enjoy peace and prosperity.
And he was really prosperous. Ten years later he began the
rebuilding of the temple as well as the rebuilding of
Caesarea, Sebaste, and other cities. His gifts to foreign
cities where Jews lived in large numbers, his building
operations in Jerusalem (in addition to the reconstruction
of the temple) and in other cities within his kingdom
marked his reign as one of real magnificence. More and
more territory was added to his kingdom either by decree
or consent of the emperor, so that in the end its extent
almost matched that of David and Solomon.

But there was another side to this royal splendor and
prosperity. Famine stalked the land from time to time. In
two different years he reduced the taxes, in the year 20 by
a third, in 14 B.C. by a quarter. Once, during the great
famine of 25-24 B.C., he sold family plate in order to provide for his starving people. The cost of his ambitious
building projects must have been enormous. It is no won-

der then that upon Herod's death, in 4 B.C., a rebellion broke out which could only be quelled by force of Roman arms under Quintilius Varus, the legate in Syria.

It is of special interest to note that now once more, as at the time of the appeal to Pompey, an embassy addressed the Romans with the plea to remove 'the kingly and other forms of human government' and let the Jews have back their ancient theocracy. The second Jewish commonwealth, founded when the exiles returned from Babylonia, had been designed to be a pure theocracy, a priestly state with no ruler other than God or his anointed representative. All that the pious Jew asked was to be let alone to worship. God in the way God had commanded, and to observe every detail of Torah as the divine law governing every aspect of life, civil as well as religious, in the holy land. But no such request could even be considered by the Romans. Their interests in Palestine required that the country be kept in close contact with the rest of the world, not shut off and isolated as a land of piety and religion, an independent theocracy or church-state in the midst of a world of busy commerce and communication, expanding culture, and constant threat of war. The age-old dream of the Jewish theocracy was destined to go down before the triumphant advance of power-politics and of the world-embracing imperium of Rome. Every event of political importance from the beginning of the second century B.C. clearly pointed in this direction. Jewish Palestine was steadily being hemmed in, overrun, crushed, and subjugated by the irresistible forces at work in the world outside. Herod had won a respite for his people, as the Maccabees had done a century before him; but at a similar cost

—for as Hellenism had been even more influential in Palestine when the Maccabees ended than when they began, so Roman penetration was even more complete when Herod died than when he began his reign.

The succession was a divided one. Archelaus became ethnarch of Judea, Idumea, and Samaria; Antipas tetrarch of Galilee and Perea, Philip tetrarch of the districts to the north and east. Antipas and Philip ruled until 39 and 34 A.D. respectively; but Archelaus was deposed and banished after ten years of misrule, and in his place a succession of imperial procurators now administered Judea and Samaria. This arrangement was interrupted for four years, when Agrippa I was king (41-44) over a territory approximately that of Herod the Great. But he died after a brief reign, and upon his death procurators were once more placed in control of Judea—each one more cruel and rapacious, if possible, than his predecessor. At last, in the year 66, the seething unrest of the nation broke out in open rebellion. After four desperate years, concluding with one of the most dreadful sieges in all history, Jerusalem fell and the temple was destroyed. The nation, ravaged and plundered and all but impotent from a war which had been doomed to failure from the start, nevertheless somehow managed to revive, and even made a second desperate and hopeless effort to regain its freedom in 132 A.D. This final revolt was completely crushed, and Jerusalem was left a heap of ruins. A Roman colony, Aelia Capitolina, was founded in its place. The temple mount was completely cleared and a pagan temple erected on the site of the ancient Jewish one. As a climax of cruelty, all Jews were forbidden to enter the city.

This long and terrible chapter in the history of ancient Judaism was the background of the life and ministry of Jesus of Nazareth. It must be obvious that, given the geographical, social, and political conditions, and the forces active in the eastern Mediterranean world during the three centuries and more from the defeat of Antiochus III at Magnesia in 190 B.C. to the final destruction of Jerusalem in 135 A.D., the ultimate outcome of the long process was inevitable. The political and economic unification of the world undertaken, perhaps at first more or less unconsciously, by Rome could have no other result than the political extinction of the Jewish nation. Judea lay in too important a position, strategically and economically, to be allowed to retain its independence. In some other part of the world, deep in the desert, hid away like Shangri-la or the kingdom of Rasselas amid inaccessible mountains, the Jews might possibly have maintained themselves, walled-off from every contact with the outside world—as legend had it the ten tribes survived in the mythical land of Arzareth (IV Ezra 13:45). Even so the lust for plunder might have led Roman expeditions to seek them out. But certainly in the situation in which Palestine actually lay there was no possibility, humanly speaking, that Roman imperialism would overlook a nation which afforded rich booty and a land that was required in the unified defense of the eastern frontier. Step by step the Roman domination increased, until eventually 'the kingdom of the Jews', free for a time under the Maccabees, half-free once more under Herod, became only the province of Syria-Palestine—and so remained as long as Roman power continued to dominate the Near East.

The ethos of that bitter, desperate time can be made out fairly well from the narrative of events in Josephus's *Antiquities,* though his written sources (for eastern affairs) have given out with the death of Herod the Great and he has to rely more upon fragmentary tradition and hearsay for the period up to the beginning of his own career as a young man just before the outbreak of the Jewish War. He 'pads' his narrative with accounts of events in Rome, Babylon, Parthia, and Adiabene; though it must not be forgotten that the picture he draws of the general situation helps to make clearer the background of the impending war. The older editors supposed that he was dependent for his knowledge of events in Rome, and especially of the assassination of Gaius and the accession of Claudius and of the share of King Agrippa I in these events, upon information provided him by Agrippa II (upon whom it has been thought he had depended for some of the material in his *Jewish War*); but since Mommsen it has generally been assumed that for these details he relied upon a Roman history, probably that of M. Cluvius Rufus.[6] Moreover the state archives were at his disposal and, as Thackeray says, were 'at his door'.

It must be remembered that Josephus's aim in writing his *Antiquities* is an apologetic one; this vast work is designed to be a convincing historical apologia for Judaism. Hence every chapter must be inspected for possible apologetic bias—though Josephus is by no means the only historian who writes 'with a purpose'! And yet the impression he conveys is on the whole no doubt a just one. It is supported not only by the few chapters which Tacitus [7] and other historians devote to eastern affairs during this interval; it is also supported and borne out by the apocalyptic and other literature from the period, and also by the traditions embodied in the gospels [8]—though the writing of social history is not one of their aims.

Judea was as helpless in the grip of Roman encirclement as any other small nation, either then or before or since, which has been caught in a similar situation. Other small nations were similarly situated at the time: e.g. the Kingdom of Commagene, where a strong pro-Roman party demanded union with the Empire. (It sounds strangely modern and central European!)

At that time Antiochus the king of Commagene died; whereupon the multitude rose up against the nobility [γνωρίμοι] and both sides sent deputations [to Rome], the well-to-do desiring to have their form of government changed into that of a [Roman] province, the multitude to be ruled by a king according to their ancestral custom. So the Senate voted to send Germanicus to settle affairs in the east.[9] (Josephus, *Antiquities* xviii.2.5 = §§ 53-54)

This was almost the same situation as that in Judea following the death of Herod, when a delegation of fifty leading Jews was sent to Rome to sue for admission to the empire. Josephus gives an extended summary of their brief.

When opportunity had been given the Jewish ambassadors to speak, those who hoped for a dissolution of kingly rule began by bringing charges against Herod's lawless ways, saying that although nominally a king he had taken to that incurable lust for authority found in every tyranny, and had used it to destroy the Jews, making whatever changes he wished upon his own arbitrary volition. . . .[10] Now the main thing they desired was to be rid of the kingly and all similar kinds of government, to be joined to [the province of] Syria and placed under the authority of the commanders [Roman legates] who were sent there. Then it would be seen whether they were really a seditious people and given to revolution or whether they would keep order if those set over them happened to be men of moderation. (Ib., xvii.11.2 = §§ 304 . . . 314)

One is strongly reminded of the idealization of Rome in I Maccabees 8:1-16 and of the Jewish response reflected in verses 17-18; evidently such idealization, perhaps justified on the whole and especially from the contrast with local misrule, was a permanent motive with one party in Palestinian politics, viz. that of the upper classes. The Jewish embassy to Rome was, we suspect (cf. § 301), made up of 'leading men' speaking on behalf of their class, whose welfare they (no doubt rightly) identified with the welfare of the nation: land-owners, we suspect, perhaps Sadducees for the most part, phil-Hellenes and pro-Romans, stout Tories in politics and religion, and firm believers in law and order. What the populace thought and hoped was another matter: Josephus traces the beginnings of anti-Roman sentiment to the taxing under Quirinius (cf. Luke 2:2; Acts 5:37), when, following Archelaus's deposition in 6 A.D., Coponius began the new Roman administration by an assessment of property. Quirinius was the imperial legate in Syria, specially charged 'to administer justice in the province and make an assessment of property'; Coponius had been sent with him to be procurator of Judea and Samaria, with plenary powers.

Moreover Quirinius himself came into Judea, which was now joined to the province of Syria, in order to make an assessment of property and to liquidate the holdings of Archelaus. Although the Jews were at first greatly disturbed over the prospect of an assessment they made no attempt to resist it, following the advice of the high priest Joazar, son of Boethus; persuaded by his words they declared their property without any hesitation. But a certain Judas, a Gaulonite from the town of Gamala, took with him a Pharisee named Saddouk and started a revolt. They claimed that this property-assessment was nothing less than the beginning of slavery, and appealed to the nation to assert its freedom; for, they said, if they succeeded it would be to their advantage through the recovery of their property; if they failed they should at least obtain the glory of proving their nobleness of spirit; moreover, they said, God preferred to help those who, having undertaken great enterprises, spared no pains in their realization. Since the rank and file listened gladly to this proposal, their bold scheme made great progress, until every kind of evil came to pass through these men and the whole nation was infected with their doctrine. . . . And so the country was filled with present evils, while the roots sank deep for troubles still to come. . . . It was chiefly the enthusiasm of the youth for this doctrine that was responsible for the nation's ruin. (Ib., xviii.1.1 = §§ 1-10)

It is strange that Judas a 'Gaulonite' (or Galilean?) should be a leader of opposition in Judea; but perhaps the term is added only to suggest his origin. It is significant that his companion at arms was a Pharisee—as over a century later Bar Kochba had as his companion and counselor the Pharisee Akiba. It was this movement which became for all Palestine the direful spring of woes unnumbered, on Josephus's view; the later rise of the Zealots was only the logical consequence and succession to this earlier uprising, inspired by the same false 'philosophy'. Poverty, despair, wild delusions of possible aid from distant lands or of direct help from heaven, utter disregard of their own safety or lives or the welfare of the nation—all this was characteristic of those fanatics who from the time of the death of Herod the Great had been spreading their ferment of unrest throughout the nation. The violent, says Josephus,

> were incapable of foreseeing the dangers they incurred. Even when they suspected them, the pleasure they were taking in the 'punishment' of those they looked upon as their 'enemies' outweighed all such considerations. Archelaus sent several persons to parley with them and bring them to a gentler frame of mind; but they would not receive them as his representatives but only as private persons speaking on their own responsibility—in fact they would not listen to anyone. The uprising was begun by those who were furiously angry and, since the multitude flocked to them, it threatened to become a large-scale revolt. (Ib., xvii. 9.2 = §§ 211-212)

It is clearly a program of coming events when Josephus describes the conditions following Herod's death.

> Thus wild and senseless folly ruled the nation, since there was no royal house to keep the multitude in order; while the foreigners who came in to quiet the rebellion only enflamed them the more by their violence and greed. (Ib., xvii.10.6 = § 277)

What about the economic situation during this dreadful period? Opinions and inferences from the scanty data vary; but it seems fairly certain that the best time, economically speaking, in the whole three centuries since the defeat of Antiochus—if we except the almost legendary 'golden age' of Queen Alexandra 76-67 B.C.—was the reign of Herod. And yet the forces at work were dangerous even then and were destined to be ruinous in the end. Palestine, like most eastern lands, indeed like most ancient countries and some modern, faced an almost continuous threat of famine. Its population rose to the very limits of the food-supply. There was no scientific agriculture, horticulture, or forestry; as far as land-cultivation was concerned, the country was still in the patriarchal stage.[11] There were no ways of stepping-up production or of otherwise increasing the prosperity of the country. Modern capitalism, with its blessing and its curse, was practically unknown in the ancient East—say east of the Provinces of Asia and Egypt. [12] Moreover the nation was steadily being drained by tribute to foreign powers. Added to this was the cost of Herod's ambitious schemes for building or rebuilding, and of his generosity to foreign cities and to the emperor. Worse than all was the rapacity of the first-century procurators, who like all the worst provincial representatives of Rome lined their own pockets at the expense of the people they were sent to govern, and made their office a word for execration and hissing.

Meanwhile, the fundamental fault lay in the two-fold taxation, civil and religious; for the religious dues were of course not remitted when the Roman tribute came to be imposed.[13] The sacred tithe, for example, continued to be paid after the Roman tithe on land was imposed in addition—not to mention other dues and duties, such as the poll tax, the house tax, customs duties (*both* import and export!—usually 5% each way), the market tax, salt tax, and other monopolies. At the *lowest,* the total taxation of Judea and Samaria in the time of Jesus must have approxi-

mated 25% of all income; and very likely it was more—
perhaps working up toward 35 or 40%.

What this meant to the peasantry and villagers of ancient Palestine can readily be imagined. If our modern
economy reaches the danger-point at 40%, with all the
resilience and resourcefulness of a capitalistic system, prospering in spite of itself because it benefits from modern
scientific production and at the same time spreads its
burdens widely by extension of credit, by open or disguised inflation, what must the burden have been to a
country like first-century Palestine, with its always narrow
and sometimes non-existent margin between production
and consumption, and unacquainted with our modern
tricks and subterfuges for staving-off evil days? There
were hungry, homeless people in multitudes, even in prosperous Galilee in the first century. And the economic in-
security of the average farmer, villager, vinedresser,
fisherman, was sufficient to explain his quick response to
anyone who offered him utopia at the end of an apocalyptic rainbow, or who suggested that the ancient theocracy
might be restored presently if only a sufficient number of
loyalists beat their pruning-hooks back into spears, their
plow-shares back into swords. As Josephus repeatedly in-
forms us, the appeal was especially strong to the younger
men. We can understand that too.

It is no doubt true that the waste and destruction of
the civil wars had set back prosperity throughout the
Roman world, not so much through the costly upkeep of
armies—after all they were not very large armies—as
through the political unsettlement of the whole eastern
Mediterranean world and through the unjust and avari-

cious administration of the provinces during the later years
of the Republic. The annual appointees of the Senate or of
the successive triumvirs certainly knew how 'to make hay
while the sun shone'. But with Augustus had come reform
and better days. Rome recouped itself speedily. What was
the point of being mistress of the known world and con-
tinuing to live in the traditional Roman simplicity, not to
say in the penury of earlier days? The great families now
lived in fabulous, almost inconceivable luxury. Even so,
the provinces responded to the upswing, following the imperial peace and the Augustan administrative reforms. The
emperors from Tiberius to Nero were no doubt liabilities
as far as the provinces were concerned; but in spite of their
negligence and derelictions prosperity steadily rose, and
under Vespasian, as later under Nerva and Trajan and
again under the Antonines, substantial advances were
made in the direction of world-wide prosperity. The architectural, artistic, literary, and other remains of that period
amply support this conclusion.

But what of Judea, Samaria, and Galilee? Luckless Palestine! There was little share for her in the rising tide of
material fortune that swept the shores of the great western
sea. Her economic life, like her political, was slowly suffocating. It was as if some oracular voice of destiny had proclaimed, 'Iudæa delenda est'. Struggle as she might, her
fate was sealed. The forces at work in the world round
about tiny Palestine were slowly but inexorably crowding
the tiny nation to the wall.

It was in such a situation that John the son of Zacharias,
the stern preacher in the wilderness, came forward with

his message of impending doom, of repentance, of baptism in the fire of divine judgment. It was in the same situation that Jesus of Nazareth announced, "The Kingdom of God is at hand."

CHAPTER VI

THE GOSPEL OF THE KINGDOM

The political and social background of Jesus' announcement of the near arrival of the Kingdom of God was one
of vast and increasing strain and tension. Nation after
nation in the Near East had been encircled, invaded, bul-
lied, or absorbed by the advancing power of Rome. By
the time of the appearance of John the Baptist, the
steady encroachment of this irresistible earthly power had
reached such a stage of completeness that only the utterly
fanatical could still hope for a restoration of Jewish independence—a kingdom of David, or even a kingdom of the
Maccabees.

There were doubtless some who saw this, and were prepared to go a long way in compromise with Rome and
even with western civilization—Hellenism—as far as political control was concerned. All they asked was to be
permitted to function religiously, to continue the round
of temple services, to study and practice the civil-reli-
gious requirements of the sacred Torah. World-empire,
the mad dream of Jewish conquest of the nations, or of an
era of Jewish world-dominion to be inaugurated super-
naturally by divine fiat—all this was utterly foreign to

their minds. True, this hope had been set forth in the Book of Daniel; but Daniel for all its influence was not yet universally recognized as scripture—and was not to be so recognized for another two generations. True, also, the age-old hope of a free nation under a Davidic king— or under the returned David himself—was embedded in the recognized scriptures of the prophets. But the realization of this hope seemed now to be indefinitely postponed. As the author of the seventeenth Psalm of Solomon had expressed it,

Raise up unto them, O Lord, their king, the son of David,
In the time that thou, O God, knowest . . . (vs. 23).

There was no certainty of the date. God's ways were past searching out—and the time was not yet. Following the decline and eventual extinction of the Maccabean dynasty, which was non-Davidic in ancestry, there had been a re-vival of nationalistic Messianism of the 'Davidic' type (reflected in these very Psalms of Solomon). But it was a short-lived revival. The Herodian house was not only non-Davidic, but even non-Israelite, an Idumean dynasty; while the rule of the procurators represented the very opposite of free nationalism—the 'wicked kingdom', 'Edom', the power of this present evil world.

In such a situation there were, politically speaking, only two possible alternatives, fanaticism and despair. The na-tion eventually chose the former of these alternatives, with the tragic result which history records—the two cap-tures of Jerusalem in 70 and 135 A.D., ending in the total extinction of the Jewish state. The other alternative, despair of political freedom, was reflected in the Saddu-

cean compromise with things as they were; these well-to-
do members and satellites of the high-priestly family were
determined to make the best of things, and enjoy the ad-
vantages of both worlds, the sacred and the secular. It is
a question if they went as far as the 'Hellenists' of pre-
Maccabean days had been willing to go; probably they did
not. They were conservatives faced with an insoluble di-
lemma, and no doubt their aim was to salvage and to
safeguard as much religious freedom as was possible under
the circumstances. It is also a question if they were the
wicked 'grafters' and 'chiselers' often described in un-
friendly modern criticism; the evidence seems to show
that they were worldly enough, but not that they were
oppressors of the poor or used their privileges as 'masters
of the temple' to exact unlawful tribute from all who
came there to worship. The Sadducean compromise was
undoubtedly a religiously motivated attempt at a solution
of the pressing problems which faced Judaism, encircled
now by aggressive and irresistible heathenism; but it was
a compromise, and it was destined to fail as completely as
the fanatical 'activism' of the Zealots.

But although, politically speaking, there were only the
two alternatives of fanaticism and despair of earthly freedom, there was still, religiously speaking, a third alternative to both, viz. the heroic 'nevertheless' of faith. Without either compromise with the actual situation or despair
of national autonomy, and without seizing the sword to
deliver a blow for God and freedom, there was still the
possibility that God himself would intervene on behalf of
Israel, right the wrongs suffered by his people, and mete

out a universal judgment upon all mankind. So would be realized at last the first and fundamental tenet of the whole Jewish theocratic conception of the world: God would 'take his great power and reign' over the nations. This had been the prophetic hope from the very beginning of Hebrew prophecy: and it explains why the prophets were as a class harbingers of doom, heralds of judgment to come (cf. Jer. 28:8). It was also the fundamental presupposition of the Torah: God had revealed himself to Israel, his chosen people; Israel had responded and voluntarily taken upon themselves to keep God's law (Exod. 24:3), to meet the divine commandments—given by God 'that a man might live, and not die' in the doing of them (cf. Ezek. 18:19). It was the basic assumption of the whole restored community after the exile, the second commonwealth. The first commonwealth had come to destruction because—as the prophets and the Deuteronomists insisted—Israel had sinned, and had failed to observe the divine requirements; but now the whole nation was resolved to keep the Law perfectly, to walk in the way God had set before them, and so to merit the divine protection and blessing.

The idea of the divine covenant, of the theocracy, of God's kingship over the whole world and his special relationship to Israel his chosen people—this was the basic presupposition of the new church-state which emerged after the exile. The first return may or may not have been 'messianic'; the reform of Ezra was unquestionably motivated by the attempt to fulfil all that God had shown to be his will. Hence the immense development of scribal teaching and authority in the centuries following. Israel was determined 'to keep the Law with its whole heart' and to please God in every way the Torah indicated. It was more than a 'legalistic' religion based upon a written code: it was the response of a devoted people to the revelation of the holy mind and loving will of their Father and King. Scribism, but also psalmody; the priestly code in the Pentateuch, but also the oldest of the synagogue prayers, e.g. the *Shemoneh Esreh;* the tithing of every field and patch of weeds, perhaps, but also the daily *Shema*—"Hear, O Israel, the Lord our God, the Lord is one; and thou shalt love the Lord thy God with all thy heart and with all thy soul and with all thy strength"— both were characteristic of the religion of Judaism, the noble theocratic religion which inspired the restoration and revival which began in the middle of the fifth century, if not at the end of the sixth, and produced the historic Judaism which the world has known ever since. It was not Ezra the scribe who laid the foundations of Judaism; it was Jeremiah the prophet.

On the basis, then, of the traditional conception of religion—or rather, of the traditional religious conception of the world and of Israel in its relation to God, as the first premise of theocratic religion—a third alternative was open to men of faith. They could trust the Most High to bring his will to pass; they could put their trust in him, and wait upon the Lord; they could pray for the final and complete coming of his Reign, and commit themselves to his salvation; they could prepare for it by repentance and obedience to his Law, and by showing loving-kindness to their neighbors; yet they need not raise a hand to force the issue, either to compel God to inter-

vene, or attempt with the puny resources of flesh and
blood to effect what in truth only God himself could
bring to pass.

Here we discover, in this third alternative, the religious-
psychological origin of that strange, weird development
of thought enshrined in the Apocalyptic Literature—in
such books as First and Second Enoch, Second Baruch,
Fourth Ezra, the Twelve Testaments, the Assumption of
Moses, and others of their genre. The religious outlook
of this literature was closely related to prophecy, though
more closely related to the later prophecy and to the
editing of the prophetic writings than to the older strain
of prophetism. For the coming judgment was still central
to its thought; and yet always, on beyond the judgment,
there lay the coming restoration, now conceived as something more than the restoration of an earthly kingdom or
of political or religious freedom and of national prosperity through the return of King David or the birth of a
scion of his fallen house. Here the whole story was transformed into a cosmic drama, and its figures were celestial,
transcendent, demonic or semi-divine. Nevertheless,
strange and bizarre as was this world-outlook of the
apocalyptists, and indebted as it undoubtedly was to foreign influences, Persian, Iranian, and other, the basic presupposition was still the traditional Jewish principle of
the divine theocracy—God's Reign over the whole world
and his special relation to Israel his chosen.

It is a question how representative of normal Judaism—
or of 'normative' Judaism, as we now say—was this
apocalyptic development. The probability seems to be that
it was far from representative of Judaism as a whole. It

was by its very nature an esoteric type of religious thought, and would be shared only by like-minded souls who belonged to special groups—in this respect somewhat like the later school of Cabbala. And yet we must not minimize its influence. The fact that different types of apocalyptic arose, with quite different sets of terminology, suggests that the literature was not limited to one group only; further, the survival of bits of apocalyptic even within the Mishna itself [1]—of all places!—proves that it was not wholly unknown in scribal circles or in the rabbinic schools; while the catastrophes of 70 and 135 A.D., with their consequent disillusionments, perhaps adequately account for the virtual suppression of this type of thought in later Jewish literature.[2]

But it was not only the apocalyptists who discovered and emphasized the religious alternative to the threatened political extinction. There were other groups in Judaism which showed—or at least sought—to find a way out of the impasse of the times. Some retreated from the world and undertook to live a life of more complete devotion to the Law. Others sought to realize Jeremiah's dream of the New Covenant, and formed an *ecclesiola in ecclesia*—the 'Zadokite' sect at Damascus, which may still have been in existence at this time. Here was a group which, having become convinced the hierarchy in Jerusalem was made up of wicked men, had sought to save their own souls by one more retirement to the desert, one more revival of nomadic simplicity (like the ancient Rechabites and others), and thus to await the Teacher whom God would send in his own good time. Others, like the Essenes, went far beyond the letter of the Law, indeed repudiated much of its letter (e.g. the requirement of animal sacrifice); and they added to their Judaism certain rules and ceremonies derived most probably from the dualistic syncretism which in those days was to be found all over the Near East—a religious theory which in general identified evil with matter, or with certain kinds of matter, and sought salvation by escape from the prison-house of the flesh. Such asceticism was not normal to Judaism; and yet asceticism was practiced here and there in Jewish circles at this time. What Philo says of the Therapeutae (in his book *On the Contemplative Life*), what Josephus tells us (in his *Autobiography*) of his teacher Bannus, what the gospels say of John the Baptist, what the apocalypses hint as the methods used by the seers in preparing for trance and vision [3]—all these data indicate that asceticism was not unknown in either Palestinian or Hellenistic Judaism of the first century.[4]

From the religious-historical and religious-psychological points of view we are confronted with phenomena which reflect the immense tensions to be found in the Jewish soul in those days. If the rise of Roman autocracy helps to account for the growth of Roman Stoicism, certainly it also helps to account for various phenomena in the religious history of the Near East as well—and particularly of Judaism, the primary tenet of whose faith was completely denied and flouted by the successful aggressions of the heathen world-empire.

Not that the political situation alone was sufficient to deny, let alone refute, the principles of the theocracy; the political situation, bad enough in itself, was also a symbol

of the whole mass of evils in this world; and the existence
and continuance of such evils constituted an even greater
denial of the sovereignty of God. The rise of Rome, the
crushing of the Jewish state, might perhaps be a stage in
the divine plan—with eventual restoration deferred but
nevertheless sure to come. Such catastrophes had been
brought to pass in the days of old, as when Assyria had
overwhelmed the kingdom of Israel. But the prophets had
interpreted all this, and had shown it to be in truth God's
punishment of Israel's sins, and had announced that after
the punishment was past Israel would be restored to divine
favor and to earthly peace and prosperity—the Assyrians
going down under the divine vengeance for their excessive
pride and cruelty and their refusal to acknowledge the
God in whose hand they were only an effective tool. But
now the situation was different, and back of the heathen
world-empire was an absolute and universal denial of
God and his purposes: Rome was only the advancing
front of a whole realm of evil; and the solution of this
problem of evil could be found, for Jewish thought, only
in terms of a temporary dualism, with a final triumph
of God and his Reign over all that exalted itself in opposition to him.[5]

Though traces of other types of solution are reflected
here and there in post-exilic Judaism, none of the classical
Greek solutions or of the Hindu was tenable for Judaism:
the envy or vindictiveness of the gods, the natural decadence of mankind, the evil of matter, the body viewed
as the tomb of the soul, the unreality of all external phenomena, the relativity of good and evil, the illusoriness of
pain and privation, human preëxistence and the inexor-

able laws governing rebirth—none of these solutions made or could possibly make any contribution to the thought of Judaism. To be acceptable by Jews the solution had to be in terms of time and of the sovereign power and wise purpose of God. Jewish thought was, in this respect, fundamentally eschatological. As conceived by the Jew, God was no aristocratic, luxurious immortal dwelling aloof from mankind like the gods of the heathen, an apathetic and indeed a cynical observer of the human comedy of folly and sin, secure in the confidence that the cyclical rotations of crime and punishment, pride and humiliation, sin and revenge, would work out the proper compensations and in the end strike the balance of justice, with penalties and awards wherever deserved. No; the God of Judaism took time seriously, took the hazards and defeats of his own purposes seriously, and would by no means acquit the guilty or overlook the oppression of the righteous. He was committed from the start to the triumph of goodness in this world—his own world, no area lying outside the divine supervision and concern: "In all their affliction he was afflicted, and the angel of his presence saved them" (Isa. 63:9). He was indeed "the high and lofty One that inhabiteth eternity"; but he "dwelt also with him that is of a contrite and humble spirit" (Isa. 57:15). Indeed, as a later rabbi stated it, "Wherever in scripture the majesty of God is mentioned, there you will also find his humility." [6]

Upon the basis of such a religious view of the world, it is no wonder that the strains and tensions of the times produced the movements we have mentioned, viz. apocalyptic and asceticism. And there is a third—the revival of prophecy. From time immemorial, political tension or danger had provided the setting for prophecy: the Philistine threat in the days of Samuel, the Syrian in the days of Elijah and Elisha, the Assyrian and Babylonian in the eighth and seventh centuries, the crisis of Judah and Jerusalem in the early sixth century, the dangers threatening the restored community in Palestine at the end of that century. And although for several centuries now no prophets had arisen—or none who had been recognized—the tension of the times once more called for prophetic utterance, and now two prophets appeared in close succession: from the wilderness of Judea, John, preaching and baptizing in the Jordan valley; and Jesus, 'the prophet of Nazareth in Galilee', preaching in the towns and villages of that district, and chiefly, it appears, in Capernaum, beside its lake. The message of the one was, put briefly, "Repent, for the Judgment is coming"; that of the other was, "Repent, for the Kingdom of God is at hand." There was a certain likeness between these two messages, as initially proclaimed; but there was a vast difference in emphasis, in spirit, and in the further unfolding of their implications.

Now it is extraordinary that Jesus' teaching regarding the Kingdom, which was central for his whole doctrine and mission, is not stated in Mark but is rather taken for granted. (This is of course additional proof that Mark is not a 'literary' creation, but a community book, written for community use and embodying community beliefs and information.) One might perhaps suspect that the reason for this absence of any statement or definition of the nature or character of the Kingdom was the well-grounded one that pagan readers in Rome or elsewhere might conclude that 'the Kingdom of God' was a political entity or group or ideal, one which threatened the security of the empire—and was therefore best left undefined. But this explanation hardly seems adequate. A far more likely view is that Mark presupposes the current collection of Jesus' sayings, 'the words and commandments of the Lord',[7] and that he only aimed to set forth in his Gospel the outward career of Jesus and his 'mighty works' as evidence that Jesus was Messiah—or 'Son of Man'—even during his earthly life and hence long preceding his resurrection and glorification, not to say his final Parousia. And yet neither Matthew nor Luke offer any statement of the nature of the Kingdom: though Matthew comes close to identifying it, on the one hand, with the Christian church and, on the other, with the final consummation lying on the other side of the Parousia, the future 'presence' ($\pi\alpha\rho ov\sigma i\alpha$) of Christ in glory. Luke adheres more closely to the Marcan view, though it is Luke's fidelity to his sources that enables us now and then to catch a glimpse of the pre-Marcan and genuinely primitive outlook of Jesus' first followers. In Paul the Kingdom has practically disappeared, in its original form, and has become something purely eschatological and transcendent: "Flesh and blood cannot inherit the Kingdom of God, nor can the corruptible inherit incorruption" (I Cor. 15:50). At the Parousia, the End, Christ "will hand over the Kingdom to [his] God and Father, when he shall have destroyed all [other] rule and authority and power: for he must reign until he [= God?] puts all enemies under his feet"—and then

God shall be 'all in all' (ib. vv. 24-28). Here the Kingdom is practically equivalent to the church, but the church not as an empirical entity made up of groups of believers; rather it is the church in its cosmic aspect, as the organ or instrument of the divine victory over evil and over 'all that opposes God' (II Thess. 2:4), instinct with all the dynamic potencies of the divine rule, 'the powers of the age to come' (Heb. 6:5). A further step is taken in the Deutero-Pauline letters (Ephesians and the Pastoral Epistles), where the church takes the place of the Kingdom—again as a supernatural entity: 'a glorious church, without spot or wrinkle or any such thing' (Eph. 5:27). In the Fourth Gospel the conception leaves even the church behind; the Kingdom is purely supernatural and transcendent, and Jesus frankly says, 'My Kingdom is not of this world' (18:36)—'my' Kingdom, be it noted, not, as in the early and certainly authentic tradition, the Kingdom of God.[8]

The New Testament shows evidence, therefore, of a steady movement away from a this-worldly conception of the Kingdom which might possibly be misunderstood in a political sense, in the direction of a purely transcendent, other-worldly conception, and resulting eventually in a diametrically opposite idea to that reflected as at least the popular hope, shared by many of Jesus' followers, in the pages of the Synoptic gospels.

How valid is this development? To what extent does it reflect at least the tendency of Jesus' own thought if not his positive teaching? At what point along the way are we to place the teaching of Jesus? Was it this-worldly or other-worldly? And was the tendency of his own mind moving in the direction followed by the early church?

The lack of definite statement which we have noted as characteristic of the Marcan and pre-Marcan tradition is a great handicap to our search for the answers to these questions. But one thing seems certain from the data of secular and sacred history alike: Jesus was put to death as a 'malefactor', as at least a potential if not active revolutionist; and he was put to death, not by the Jews but by the Roman governor of Judea. It may have been at Jewish instigation; but the fact is certain that he was crucified, not stoned to death [9]—the penalty he suffered was Roman, not Jewish: it was the penalty of criminal slaves, robbers, and revolutionists. Even the inscription on the cross, it has been suggested, may not be accurately reported: the claim to be 'king of the Jews' may be so stated from apologetic motives, just as the claim to be 'Son of Man' is adapted to purposes of apologetic and given its setting in the Jewish 'trial'. But 'king' was a term of wide range in that day and in that part of the world; and any 'king' of a band of brigands, if put to death by the Roman authority, would as likely as not be described as 'king of the Jews' by Pilate and his men. Pilate, like other procurators, had a perfect contempt for the people he governed and would not spare their feelings. Without assuming then that the account of Jesus' own personal claim to be 'king of the Jews' is authentic, and granting that it may reflect later interpretation of the scene, it is certain that Jesus was put to death as the head of a movement which Pilate was persuaded might prove dangerous—not to Jewish interests, but to Roman; and not merely to law and order but to the security of the Roman hold upon southern and central Palestine. From a purely historical, non-theological point of view, this seems to be the most probable explanation of the motives at work in the tragedy; and it is the motive clearly set forth in the special tradition of Luke, whether or not he was at this point following some written document or other, L or L² or a special Passion Narrative, or only additional oral tradition (Luke 23:2, 5, 14-15). As we have already observed in Chapter I, this view is the more probably derived from tradition in that it states one of the charges against Christians which the author is refuting throughout Luke-Acts: Pilate's repeated affirmation of Jesus' innocence would scarcely offset, in the eyes of Greek or Roman inquirers, the fact that Pilate eventually put him to death when he could easily have saved him. This is *more* than an apologetic foil for Pilate's efforts to spare our Lord: it represents genuine tradition.

The Kingdom of God, the central subject of Jesus' teaching, could therefore, according to his earliest opponents, be interpreted in a political sense. In other words, it was a this-worldly, not other-worldly, object of hope, faith, devotion, and loyalty. From such a beginning we can readily see how the tendency to 'spiritualize' and reinterpret it might proceed, and actually did proceed, in the course of the Christian mission as reflected in successive stages of the writing of the New Testament. But it is difficult, on the other hand, to see how a purely spiritual, transcendental conception could be so crassly misinterpreted as to make it a promise of earthly empire, with thrones, tables, a treasury, and all the trappings of 'temporal' rule.

But to Jesus a Kingdom of God to be set up or realized in this world meant none of these things, either political power or the outward trappings of royalty. If there is anything he did not wish to be, it was an earthly king— 'king of the Jews' or emperor of the whole *orbis terrarum*. His views could be represented by others as involving such a claim—e.g. the Davidic Messiahship; but it was not his expectation or claim. His own view was too completely and exclusively theocratic for such a compromise with the dynasts of this earth and their great ones: it was not his own kingdom he was talking about but the Kingdom of *God*. This idea was a revival, in Jewish thought: the term 'Kingdom of God' scarcely occurs in the literature of Judaism immediately prior to Jesus;[10] while the concept, as set forth in his teaching, has a distinctive set of connotations all its own. It is not the Kingdom of the future, but the eternal Reign of God over his people; nor is it limited, as in certain rabbinic passages, to the practice of religion or the saying of the Shema, but is the world-wide, transforming consequence of God's actual and active Kingship over his creation. Hence sin and evil, suffering and disease, in fact everything that stood in the way of God's complete rule must be abolished and brought to naught (I Cor. 15:24)—was, indeed, already being destroyed as the world was being brought into subjection once more to the divine rule.

In this view the Kingdom, i.e. the Kingship, belonged solely to God. There was no room for a messianic king; and to claim kingship for any human being, for example for himself, would have been to deny the central emphasis in all his teaching, viz. the direct, immediate control of the universe and of every event and incident in it by God himself with his unlimited power, love, and mercy. This is a hard saying, and seems at first glance to undermine orthodox Christology, at least as orthodox Christology is formulated these days. But Christology has another and better foundation and can be adequately supported apart from the naïve, if primitive, identification of Christ with the King of Israel, or of Christ's 'kingdom' or 'kingship' with the Kingdom and Kingship of God. To put it plainly, for Jesus to claim himself to be the head of God's Kingdom, after all he had said in his public teaching about the divine rule, would have been nothing short of blasphemy.

The declension, in popular interpretation, was swift and simple: if there is—or is to be—a kingdom, Jesus must be the king, whether actually or in anticipation. But the inference was mistaken. In Jesus' teaching the earthly realization of the Kingship of God left no room for an earthly king, or for any other king but God himself. This had been the burden of Hebrew prophecy from the beginning. Jesus' doctrine was the purest form of theocracy, with no accommodation to popular ideas of a restored Davidic empire or for the dream, denied by the later Maccabees and the Herods, of a revived monarchy under an anointed ('Messiah') of the Lord all their own. It is the ideal of theocracy, i.e. the direct and exclusive Rule of God without human intermediaries; it is the same idea that breathes in many of the most exalted passages of the Old Testament, in the Psalter and the Prophets and even in earlier writings than these; and it also occurs in many a passage of the rabbinic writings.

The principle might be thought anarchic, though it was

deeply rooted in the Orient and especially among the Semites. It had survived for centuries, and lay behind more than one revolt against earthly sovereigns and their kingdoms, from the days of the Persian 'Great King' and long before.[11] And it clearly underlies Jesus' reply to the question regarding the Tribute Money.

They sent Pharisees and partisans of Herod to him in order to find a charge against him from his own words. They came and asked him, "Master, we know that you are sincere and do not speak to please your hearers. You make no display of oratory but proclaim the divine teaching honestly. Must one pay tribute to the Roman emperor, or not? Shall we pay, or withhold it?" But recognizing their hypocrisy he replied, "Why bring the question to me? Hand me a denar, so I can look at it." They did so, and he asked, "Whose picture is this, and whose writing?" They answered, "Caesar's." And he said to them,
"Then give to Caesar what belongs to Caesar,
And to God what belongs to God."
(Mark 12:13-17) [12]

It was this ancient traditional doctrine of the divine Kingship, always implicit in Hebrew religious thought and often explicit, that Jesus brought to its highest expression. In other words, he took in simple earnest the fundamental doctrine of revealed religion, and in his teaching and ministry and in his own life and character gave to it the most perfect elucidation and illustration the world has ever seen. It is God's Kingdom, God's Reign, not the kingdom or reign of some anointed representative of God, which is Jesus' great and continual concern: and certainly it is no dream of his own personal dominion over the nations that interests him and forms the subject of his teaching.

Here is the point of departure for any genuinely satis-
factory Christology, for any truly orthodox doctrine of
the Incarnation: not the 'claims' of Christ,[13] read back
into his life and utterances by later apologetics and devotion, but the actual realization in this world, under the
conditions of a particular time and place, of the presence
and the power, the love and the mercy of the eternal God.
It is the *spirit* of Christ, the most real thing in man's whole
upward reach toward God, in God's downward reach toward man, that justifies the attribution to Jesus of all the
titles by which orthodox Christianity has tried to shadow
forth something of his uniqueness, of the splendor of God
manifest in the face of Christ Jesus our Lord.[14] It must
be understood that these titles were religiously conferred,
first of all, as acts of faith and worship, not of metaphysical speculation or of historical reminiscence. The
only meaning they have is religious. Hence to take them
out of their religious setting, in devotion and liturgy, in
prayer and communion, and treat them as entries in a
purely historical account, is grossly to misconstrue them;
they cannot even be explained in their full wealth of
meaning and connotation under such treatment.

What then was Jesus' conception of the Kingdom of
God?—We have delayed the answer to this question,
raised in an earlier lecture and indeed involved in this
whole course, in order to take into consideration various
factors which are required for an adequate answer. Even
so, we have not considered them all, but only a few which
are less commonly considered at the present day—e.g. the
political and social situation in Palestine at the time—on

the theory that if these should prove adequate it will not be necessary to appeal to other factors whose importance is less certain, indeed whose very existence is questionable. I refer to the hypothesis of widespread popular interest in the apocalyptic literature as a cause of public unrest, and the modern assumption that in the first century there was a universal expectation of the immediate appearance of the Messiah. So far as we are able to make out, the apocalypses were the esoteric literature of an insignificant minority, and had little influence upon the nation as a whole. Moreover, as Klausner [15] and other experts have assured us, the figure of the Messiah was always conceived politically, i.e. as an anointed king who should reign in God's name and with the divine blessing over a restored Israel. Were this not so, and had the Messiah been generally conceived in transcendental ('apocalyptic') terms—e.g. as 'the Son of Man' in the Visions of Enoch—it is difficult to see how Judaism could have avoided the substitution of the transcendental for the earthly Messiah after the two national catastrophes of 70 and 135 A.D., somewhat as the Christians had already done in identifying Jesus of Nazareth with the transcendental 'Son of Man'. If it be said that the second-century Jewish conception of the Messiah is due to revulsion from the political events identified with these two tragic dates in Palestinian history, this is the answer: The Messiah was simply inconceivable by the majority of Jews as a transcendental, supernatural, angelic and purely other-worldly figure. The figure that survived the political catastrophes was still a political figure. That simple fact surely has more significance than has been recognized in it hitherto.

Far from being purely transcendental and other-worldly, Jesus' conception of the Kingdom of God was, as far as we can make out from the basic tradition under-lying the gospels, that of the Reign of God to be realized completely upon the soil of Palestine, the holy land. Its center was to be here, but its influence would reach to the ends of the earth and 'many shall come from east and west, from north and south,' to share in its blessings. Jerusalem was to be in truth the city of the 'Great King', the capital of the whole earth. The conditions of human life would be changed and made to correspond to the requirements of the divine King—though Jesus' emphasis was not upon the celestial bliss of those who were to be called (or to be raised from the dead) in order to share its blessings: his emphasis was all but exclusively upon the ethical and religious conditions of entrance into the King-dom. In a word, Jesus' 'theology' and 'eschatology' are derived, not from the apocalyptic literature with its wholly visionary circle of ideas, but from the Law, the Prophets and the Psalms of the Old Testament. His teach-ing regarding the Kingdom is not a further elaboration of the doctrines of the Book of Enoch or the Testaments of the Twelve Patriarchs: it is the old doctrine of the theocracy, fundamental to all Jewish thought since the days of the prophets and made the real constitution of the commonwealth after the exile. It is an earthly King-dom, Jewish—yet international in aim and purpose; ac-knowledging no king but God—and yet diametrically op-posed to all programs of violence like that of the Zealots; at basis a purely religious conception, unaffected by the political and social turmoil of the time—and yet (since

Jesus' following was widespread) open to misinterpretation as a plan for revolution, probably very largely because its central term and idea were also those of the pro-
tagonists of popular liberties: 'God and his Reign', 'no
king but God', 'the ancient liberties of the people of God'.

The teaching of Jesus, let me repeat, can only be described from our point of view as purely religious, not
political or economic or as setting forth a program for
social reform. This is stated of course as we use these
terms; though for ancient Jewish thought, 'religion' embraced all of life and had consequences in every sphere of
human interest and activity, so much so that ancient
Judaism had no specific term for 'religion' but only de-
scriptive words for various religious activities: faith, or
faithfulness, righteousness, truth, loving-kindness, patience, obedience, waiting upon the Lord, and so on. Nor
was Jesus' teaching theological, as opponents of 'the social
gospel' often assume, and as neo-Calvinists and others try
to prove, reading Pauline and even Augustinian ideas back
into his sayings. He was a Jewish teacher of religion, a lay
teacher, unaccredited by the religious authorities, neither
a priest, a scribe, nor a rabbi; and yet he taught with
unquestionable authority, speaking like a prophet by
direct inspiration and command the words of the Most
High. His message was continuous with the divine revelation contained in the Old Testament, and brought it to its
highest culmination; in his presence men were conscious
of the same Voice which spoke in the Law and the Prophets of the holy Covenant. He was an *ancient* Jewish
teacher, and there was no suggestion of modernity about

him.[16] And yet his gospel is timeless, an 'eternal gospel' (Rev. 14:6), and he speaks 'over the heads of his contemporaries' to all generations of men, in all races, in all ages. Once, in the long files of human history, once, among the unnumbered millions of human beings who have peopled this earth since our species emerged, the Perfect Man appeared; once, and once only, the contact was made, the proper focus was achieved, the accurate and completely trustworthy transmission of the Person, the Word, the Voice of the Eternal was effected. This we are compelled to believe was no result of chance but the work of divine initiative, the Act of the living God of Israel, who is above and outside human history and yet moves mysteriously and positively within it to effect his purposes. It is only the later Greek way of describing all this to say God was 'incarnate' in Jesus of Nazareth; but the faith in the divine initiative is present in the Christian movement from the first. The very oldest traditions contain it, e.g. Acts 10:36f:

The word (τὸν λόγον) which *God sent* to the sons of Israel, preaching peace through Jesus Christ . . . the movement (τὸ γενόμενον ῥῆμα) that took place all over Judea . . . how *God anointed him* with holy Spirit and power . . .

It is a long way from that simple, inchoate faith to the involved terminology of the later Catholic creeds; but the route is fairly direct.

Jesus was, as Paul said, 'a minister of the circumcision' (Rom. 15:8), no Hellenistic wise man, founder of a cult, political leader or reformer, or prophet of a strange god. The Kingdom he announced was nothing new or strange either, but age-old, and known to all Jews of the time as the basic idea of their religion. This is the real reason why Jesus does not explain its meaning and differentiate his conception from that of others: there is no need to do so, for his conception is that of the Old Testament scriptures and of Judaism generally, but widened, deepened, enriched with a new spirit and outlook, and set over against the narrow legalism of one school and the bitter fanaticism of the other, among the contending parties whose influence counted for most with the 'people of the land' in Jesus' day.

Under the conditions of that time there would have been no meaning in any distinction between 'social', 'political', or 'religious' ideas: all were subsumed under the concept of the theocracy, God's Reign over his people and over his world as a whole. In our day we may think the situation is different, and that under present conditions, in a modern and non-Jewish environment, the principles of Jesus' teaching can be applied only in terms of the social gospel. That is no doubt true, to a large extent; and yet we may question how far a piecemeal application is going to succeed—the new patch on the old garment, once more! What is really needed in our distracted world is a complete submission of human motives to the will of God, a complete and radical renovation of human society, re-fashioning it upon the principle of faith in the righteous-ness of God and a determination to live in accordance with his revealed purposes. That was Jesus' program—or 'proposal', as John Hutton called it [17]—for the tortured, distracted, chaotic world in which he lived; and it is still his proposal, for ours.

Is it too simple a program? Would we like something more in accordance with modern sociology or psychology or political theory? No matter what we would like, this proposal is the only one which has ever in any measure succeeded, even on the small scale upon which it has been tried by various groups here and there. Its simplicity lies only in its formulation; it becomes complex enough when applied, and in collision with the age-old, deeply rooted habits, customs, and attitudes of human beings. Perhaps, with the crisis of today upon us, we might do well to postpone the further discussion of it from the purely academic, theoretical point of view, and try to get it applied practically, before it is too late.

Chapter VII

THE GOSPEL IN THE NEW TESTAMENT

Surprising as it may seem, modern New Testament scholarship is coming to the view that the teaching of Jesus was purely and simply religious. We were not prepared for this. We had thought he might be a social reformer, and his Gospel of the Kingdom of God another plan for utopia—which men could bring into effect as soon as they became sane enough, altruistic enough, intelligent enough to work for each other's good rather than harm. Or we had supposed he might be an ethical philosopher, a Greek sage in disguise, announcing a principle of universal brotherhood and of divine-human sonship which should help to clear up the remaining problems of conduct, public and private, and strike the fine balance of less and more, of advantage and disadvantage to society from the behavior of the individual, of the claims of private welfare against the demands of the state or of society generally. Or perhaps he was an institutionalist, the founder of a movement, the institutor and organizer of the church with its regular ministry and order of worship and sacraments, its plan for the evangelization of the world, its rules and regulations governing the lives of its members. Or possibly, as many have held during the past thirty years, he was none of these, but instead was an out-and-out apocalyptist, a 'thorough-going' eschatologist, who believed—and announced—the impending end of the world, and bade men prepare for this event by the most rigorous and heroic measures of self-sacrifice, abandonment of property, renunciation of rights, voluntary poverty, and even a considerable degree of emotional if not physical self-mutilation (e.g. Matt. 19:12). Of course his ethics, on this view, was 'interim ethics'. Understood literally, and applied literally, his doctrine of renunciation of family life would have produced a generation of celibates, and with that the end of the family—and of human society. But the danger was not serious; long before this fatal eventuality was ever realized, the Judgment Day, the Resurrection, the inauguration of the New Age should have taken place, and men and women should be ἰσάγγελοι —'neither marrying nor being married but like the angels in heaven' (Mark 12:25, Luke 20:35-36).

None of these views is defensible today. We must admit of course (1) that there are elements in the gospels which, if taken in isolation and separated from the rest, seem to warrant each of these alternative interpretations. But they cannot all be true—since they neutralize and cancel one another. Nor can any one of them be true—since each is confronted by other materials in the gospels which cannot be so interpreted. There are too many intractable elements in the tradition to permit us to hold any one of these views and to represent Jesus as either a social reformer, an ethical philosopher, the founder of an institution, or an apocalyptic enthusiast. These are all interpretations, and forced interpretations at that.

We must also acknowledge (2) that there were interpretations of Jesus from the very beginning, even before the Christian movement got outside Palestine. The Hellenistic world—chiefly outside Palestine—of course did its best to explain him in its own terms. The long struggle over Christology from the second century to the sixth is in large measure the result of the effort made by the Graeco-Roman world to envisage Jesus in terms with which it was familiar and which it could interpret and use. The formula finally adopted was that of Incarnation —an idea which to Jesus himself and his apostles, being Jews, would have been impossible if not incomprehensible. —But there was interpretation (of an earlier kind) even on the Jewish, the Palestinian, the Galilean level of the tradition. The basic material which scholars label 'Q' and 'L' and 'M', and the substratum of tradition in Mark, not to mention a small nucleus of historical element in John— these traditions are Jewish, Palestinian, Galilean in origin. And there is variety of interpretation even here: according to L, the special Lucan cycle of tradition, Jesus is a prophet; in M, the special document of Matthew, he is a teacher and controversialist, a lawgiver, even a second Moses; in the 'Old Stories' [1] in Mark he is represented as a healer and teacher; in another stratum he is the Jewish Messiah in an almost purely nationalistic sense; while in still another stratum of Mark and in parts of Q, he is the future celestial 'Son of Man'.[2] These interpretations are obviously older than the Hellenistic, Graeco-Roman interpretations which the later gospels and the rest of the New

Testament set forth—not to mention their patristic, mediaeval or modern elaborations and the inventions of still
other and more recent categories.

Now there is something to be said for all this variety of
interpretation: Jesus was more, not less, than all these
diverse representations; his teaching contained more, not
less, than all these various inferences.

The person of Jesus was too great to be fully expressed in
terms of Messiahship and the coming Kingdom, and soon burst
through the categories of that early faith. . . . Every one of
the terms in which men have tried to set forth the person and
work of Jesus—Messiah, Son of Man, Son of God, Sacrifice,
Passover, Lamb of God, Logos—so far from making Jesus more
intelligible to us than He is without them, needs interpretation
today. "These are the accounts that men have given of Jesus
Christ, and He has been more than they. He has transcended,
He has gone through one picture of Him and another, one
description and another: He has been more, far more, than any
of these conceptions, taken by themselves or taken together,
have been able to represent. They are inadequate, and there is
He, the great fact." [3]

He was so great, his significance for the life of men was
so important, that none of these interpretations was adequate. And since he was unique, it is no wonder that men
strove in various ways to grasp him, to classify him, and
to account for him; and no wonder, either, that in the
end their categories proved inadequate and failed. He is
the most interesting, the most attractive, the most in-
triguing figure, to say no more, that our world has ever
known. His teaching, brief as is the record of it in the
New Testament, is the most fertile source of religious and
ethical inspiration that has ever influenced our human race.

The problem facing the student of the gospels is one that arises out of the very conditions under which the tradition regarding Jesus, his works and his teachings, was handed down. It was a social possession from the outset.[4] And since all history, including oral tradition, involves interpretation, it was inevitable that those who handed down the accounts of Jesus' deeds and teachings should describe him as they understood him, either as prophet, teacher, scribe, Messiah, or Son of Man. Our problem, as set for us by the results of a century of critical New Testament scholarship, is to find if possible the point from which these divergent Christologies set out, the point of divergence of the whole range of New Testament and early Christian interpretation of the person of Jesus. And we shall need to proceed warily, since the records have been edited, not only as they appear in the written gospels but even during the oral period that preceded.

That point of divergence, the earliest conception of Jesus' person, calling and work, is the conception of a religious teacher, 'a prophet, and more than a prophet', who lived so close to God that his religious convictions were uttered with a divine authority; so close to God that his 'mighty works' were viewed even by himself as the activities of the Spirit of God; so close to God that in his own person and in the group about him he—and they— saw the Reign of God already realized and present. Instead of inaugurating something new, after the modern fashion, he and his message and his activities fitted simply and easily into the frame of ideas provided by traditional Judaism, the religion of the divine covenant or theocracy. There was certainly newness, uniqueness enough about him; but it was the newness, the uniqueness of inner quality, not of outward form. He was no modern reformer, psychologist, or ethical philosopher—let alone a fanatical Jewish apocalyptist. His criticism of the Law and of the tradition was the criticism of a Jew—almost of a Pharisee. His healings were restorations of 'children of Abraham' to their rightful state, free from the oppressions of Satan. His attitude toward the Romans was courageous but cautious—one which a Sadducee might almost have commended, had he not said so much more that seemed to disturb the *status quo* and looked quite away from the scheme of things cherished by that group.

There was nothing of the flaming social radical about him; the spirit of Judas the Galilean who headed an armed revolt 'at the time of the assessment' was utterly foreign to the spirit and attitude of this other and greater Galilean. Even the saintly Akiba, who supported the revolt of Bar Kochba early in the second century and died a martyr at the downfall of that ill-starred undertaking, had little in common with Jesus of Nazareth. Both these leaders, Judas and Bar Kochba, the one two decades prior to the public career of Jesus, the other more than a century later, headed movements that may perhaps in some sense be called 'messianic'; both undertook to do something 'practical' to meet the issues of the time. But Jesus had no program of direct action to offer—surely none with this type of 'practicality'. If Jesus taught, as I think he did, a doctrine of complete and unqualified pacifism, we can certainly understand it. No other course was open to any sane man in his time. Only ignorant fanatics could dream of another war for Jewish independence. Unfortunately, the policy of the fanatics prevailed, and the revolt begun in the year 66 was crushed after one of the most hopeless wars in all history. It is a mark not only of the religious spirit of Jesus but of his intellectual insight that he saw clearly the futility of any resort to the sword.

Nor, on the other hand, was he a pale, impractical dreamer, voicing a fantastic and impossible hope or urging his followers to a course of merely private renunciation and self-preservation. In a feverish and fanatical generation, which was dissatisfied with everything and ready to follow any program that promised deliverance, however fantastic, he was the coolest, sanest, most practical of all the—really few—practical men of our race.[5] And he lived in a world which was not unlike our own. For over two hundred years, as we have seen, since a Roman army defeated Antiochus III at Magnesia, the whole Near East had trembled at the steady advance of the western Republic. Historians may of course hold—with Mommsen—that Rome had no plan, had never intended to overrun the nations of Asia Minor, the Levant, Syria, Palestine, and Egypt. Perhaps so; but the fact remains that Rome could not have advanced more steadily and consistently, or more ruthlessly and irresistibly, had she followed a settled policy, and had the *Drang nach Osten* been a dinner-table topic or the subject of discussion at every army-camp for two centuries. When Jesus began his ministry this phase of the political evolution of the Near East was entering its final stage. Jewish Palestine was all but completely encircled, and had already lost most of its independence. Forty years later came the siege of Jerusalem; sixty-five years after that, the total destruction of Jerusalem as the Jewish world-center. Humanly—i.e. politically—speaking, the situation was as hopeless for Judaism and for the Jewish state as was that of Czecho-Slovakia in 1938 or that of Poland in 1939. There was absolutely no hope whatever of a successful resort to arms. And Jesus saw this as clearly as if he had been a Roman or a Greek. He lived in the world of realities, not the dream-world of apocalyptic visions and hallucinations.

And yet his motive was not that of political submission —such a motive as moved Seneca the Stoic court-philosopher, or the later Boethius, or any man who has recognized the futility of opposition either to a tyrant or to a world-power crazed with lust for more territory and for absolutely autocratic, dictatorial control. He was something *more* than a pacifist, and saw the world with his eyes wide open. What the times called for was not quietism and inaction, but positive peace-making. "Blessed are the peace-makers . . ." (Matt. 5:9). His Gospel of the Kingdom of God, we might almost say, was his practical program for meeting the crisis of his day. And it is one that is good for every crisis, in every age: if it succeeds, it will solve the problems of the whole world quite as adequately as those of every individual. The Gospel of the Kingdom, as John Hutton truly said,[6] was 'the proposal of Jesus': a genuinely practical proposal to meet the urgent need of his own time as of all times. For it involved justice, forbearance, mutual recognition, and it put God and the human soul above every kind of social or economic advantage.

If ever a peace society is formed which will take *this* as its program and get beyond the debatable minutiae of personal conduct, e.g. the duty or otherwise of non-resistance as a purely human instrument of political action, on a par with the strike in embattled industry; and will take seriously the fundamental causes of war, which are economic, political, and psychological, instead of vainly crying, 'Peace, peace', when there is no peace; and will work harder for social and political justice than for private satisfaction of conscience; then there are surely many of us who will join that society with enthusiasm and support its propaganda with all our hearts.

But do we not already belong to such a peace society?— one whose founder was Jesus himself, but whose efforts have so far failed, very largely because it has not held firmly to its central mission which is to proclaim the Gospel of the Reign of God, and because it has compromised too often with the injustices that make for war— the very thing it is meant to oppose? Too much of our preaching against war is directed against war alone, as if it were the sole evil; whereas the real evil is the injustices, lies, and tyrannies that lead to war.

The message of Jesus, we have said, was purely and simply religious. Its fundamental presupposition was the ancient theocratic principle: God is the King of all the earth; God is the true and only King of Israel; and yet there are conditions in the world—and in Israel—which are incompatible with God's perfect Reign. Hence, in a very true sense, God's Reign must 'come': it is not yet fully realized, for his will is not yet obeyed perfectly upon earth as it is in heaven. These evils in the world must be done away before God's Kingship can fully come to pass. Men can coöperate in this, as by repentance and works of righteousness; though they cannot conceivably 'set up' or 'bring about' God's Reign—God is no democratically chosen leader of the universe, but its Eternal King, who must himself 'take his great power and reign'. But the forces of the divine Reign are already astir, 'the powers of the age to come' are already at work. Jesus' own ministry was evidence of this—his healing of the sick and his exorcism of demons: "If I by the finger of God cast out demons, then is the Kingdom of God come upon you" (Luke 11:20). When his disciples returned from a brief but successful mission to the neighboring villages, so the evangelist relates, Jesus rejoiced in spirit and exclaimed, "I beheld Satan fallen as lightning from heaven" (Luke 10:18). The setting may be 'editorial' and artificial, but the saying surely sounds authentic. In some sense the Kingdom was already present, was already in process of full realization. What were Jesus' plans for the further extension of his mission, using his disciples as helpers and 'messengers' to Israel, and then perhaps even beyond the borders of Israel—this we shall never know.[7] His life was cut short in the midst of his days, by the worst tragedy that has ever come to the human race.

There has been considerable discussion, recently, of the sense in which Jesus assumed the Kingdom to be already present. Professor C. H. Dodd [8] and others have advanced the theory known as 'realized eschatology', based in part upon a translation of Mark 1:15, as "The Kingdom of God has come." [9] The difficulty with this view is threefold, at least. (1) The translation is strained: ἤγγικεν ordinarily means, 'has come near at hand', 'has come close'. Of course it is simply not 'is drawing near', as our 'thorough-going eschatologists' would have it. Moreover, (2) a 'realized' eschatology of this kind leaves no room for the final judgment—the Kingdom has arrived without any preceding divine judgment: and how was such an idea possible in first century Judaism whether apocalyptic or not? Again, (3) such a theory appears to do less than justice to those elements in the gospel tradition which stress the future realization of the purpose of God, the reward of the righteous, the blessings upon the faithful—as e.g. in the Beatitudes. (4) A further difficulty lies in the historical situation thus set up: The death of Jesus was tragic enough on the futuristic theory—how could the faith of his followers possibly have survived that catastrophe if they had assumed the Kingdom to be already realized in Jesus' lifetime?

And yet, for all these objections, there is a great truth at the heart of this idea. In one sense, the Kingdom—i.e. the Reign of God—was already realized: God was King from everlasting, and his Reign had had no beginning— his Kingdom was an eternal Kingdom, from the beginning of creation and before. Further, the full and final realization of God's reign upon this earth was to be seen already taking place in the ministry of Jesus. In Jesus and his band of followers, the Kingdom was already present: as Dibelius says,[10] Jesus and his movement were 'the sign' the Pharisees requested but failed to recognize. In a true sense, Jesus was the Bearer, the Bringer of the Kingdom—but not in the dramatic apocalyptic sense of the supernatural last judgment of all the world. The coming of the Kingdom was like a solar transit, or the dawn of a new day: the sun was risen, and therefore the day was really here; but the full realization of the sun's presence, the complete occlusion and obliteration of all lesser luminaries and of the ancient dark which still blinded men's eyes—all that still lay in the immediate future, which should soon be present, which was already giving way to the present.

Prophecy always foreshortens the future; prophets always live proleptically, as much at home in tomorrow as in today, since they see everything in terms of a process, i.e. the realization of the divine will.[11] Our neatly distinguished past, present, and future had much less cogency for the prophetic type of mind. In the view of the prophet, time was a steady flow, and past slipped into present and present into future without a break. Indeed, it may even be more than the prophetic type of mind we are faced with here: the ordinary Semitic outlook upon this moving scene is one for which past and future are not sharply contrasted, one as the unreal and the other as the possible, but in a sense coexist and are mutually convertible—the very forms of the verb in Hebrew grammar suggest this quality of mind. It is therefore more or less needless to discuss what is implied by the verb in the Beatitudes: 'for theirs *is* the Kingdom of Heaven'—does it mean 'is now, in the present', or 'will be, in the future'? And what is implied when no verb is used at all, as in Matthew 5:12? Equally, each Beatitude pronounces a blessing upon those who are—or are to be—persecuted, gentle, poor in spirit, since the blessing, fully to be realized in the future, is even now appropriated by those upon whom it is pronounced. Such people do not have to wait to be rewarded, at some time or other in the future; their reward is already realized, has already begun, even in the midst of the most untoward and most contradictory conditions of outward existence. Already they share the victory of the coming Reign.

This is characteristic not only of the central thought of the Kingdom but also of Jesus' ethics as a whole. Take again for example one of the Beatitudes which, though attested only in Matthew, is surely authentic and sufficiently represents Jesus' whole attitude:

> Blessed are the peace-makers;
> For they shall be called sons of God.
> (Matthew 5:9)

Peace-*makers!* This means something more than being peaceably inclined, or willing to live at peace, or to grant or to accept forgiveness and reconciliation with one's neighbors. Like all the Christian virtues, this is active not passive, positive not negative, objective rather than subjective, creative rather than submissive. It is a total misreading of Christian ethics to make the acceptance of life's ills, or the renunciation of earthly good or submission to the inevitable, the central or dominant note in Christian character. Traces of that attitude may of course be found here and there in Christian history and literature; and those whose familiarity with Christianity is limited to some relatively small area of Christian piety may perhaps think themselves justified in describing Christian ethics as 'a morality for slaves', not for freemen—just as, from another point of view, pacifists are inclined to identify the Gospel as a whole with pacifism. But you cannot force the New Testament into that formula, nor early Chris-

tianity as a whole, nor Christianity as a total historical phe-
nomenon through the centuries since its birth. Christianity
encouraged martyrdom. Yes; but only as a means to an
end; and the martyrs are always celebrated, in hymns and
liturgy, as victors, not as victims.

> Now they sit in heavenly glory,
> Now they reign with Christ their king.

Christian virtue is not the line of least resistance—but of
most resistance. The victors are those who fell where the
fight was hottest—that is the paradox of Christian sanc-
tity. Not retreat, not world-flight, not the sanest and least
uncomfortable *modus vivendi* in a world which at best is
none too comfortable—that is Epicureanism, not the Gospel of Christ and his saints.

This is the essential presupposition of all our Lord's
ethics: life in and for the Kingdom of God is both a present possession and a future reward. Is is the anticipation
of his Reign, and at the same time it is the realization that
it already exists. It is 'to come'—and yet it has always
existed; it is both coming and it has already come in the
sense that God the King is himself already subduing a
rebellious province, man's will and the wicked world
resulting from human or demonic disobedience. Life in the
Kingdom is thus *both* a present possession and a future
reward: for it means sharing in the conquest now which
is leading to the victory hereafter. It is no question of
either-or, with some uncertainty attaching to the future:
for the follower of Jesus already lives by the principles
which must prevail when God's will is perfectly done
upon earth. And yet this is only another way of saying

that he lives by the principles which reflect God's will from the beginning of creation. For the Kingdom that is to be is only the full realization here upon earth of the Reign of God which is from everlasting.

Hence the social teaching of Jesus, and the ethics of the New Testament as a whole, are not some merely prudential set of rules for the guidance of individuals who find themselves in the midst of an evil and naughty world—'interim ethics' for the guidance of the few elect during the brief interval to precede the Last Judgment and the final consummation. On the contrary, they are grounded in the very nature of things, which is—as Augustine said—the expression of the will of God. The ethics of the Gospel find their sanction upon no lower level than the eternal purpose of God, which, so the Bible conceives it, reflects the very nature of God.[12] To 'enter' and share God's Kingdom, one must be like God, reflecting in daily practice the benevolence, the wisdom, the patience, the mercy and loving-kindness of the Eternal. "Ye therefore shall be perfect, as your heavenly Father is perfect" (Matthew 5:48)—this is no metaphysical theory, but the simplest and most comprehensive statement of the whole ethical outlook and demand of Jesus.

It is clear then that the 'social' teaching of Jesus is no misnomer: these demands are not limited to private practice, as if one could be a member of the Kingdom, as of some secret society, in isolation and without regard to the whole group, community, nation, or world in which one lives. They must inevitably be put in practice on the large scale of society generally, since this is God's world, not the devil's. How that is to be done is not defined in advance.

Christianity has no set of blue-prints for the building of utopia; but it has a motive, the motive without which neither utopia nor even the blue-prints for its construction would have either meaning or possibility. The details of its realization are left to men who have accepted this motive, and live in the present world as members of God's universal Kingdom that both is and is to be. Nor, by the same token, can the new patch be stitched to the old garment (Mark 2:21)—by a limited application of Christian ethics to certain specified areas of human conduct, while conceding at the same time that society as a whole, or certain large areas of human concern, e.g. the relations between nations, must be left to the operation of other principles, say those of selfishness, materialism, or the ungovernable biological urges that sweep into human life from really sub-human levels. If Jesus' ethics are to be followed and applied at all, they must be followed and applied consistently; for they are the ethics that flow from the Reign of God himself over his world.

There are some very important further questions: How was it possible for the teacher of such doctrines to be put to death as a seditionist or revolutionary? And why does the New Testament as a whole lay so much emphasis upon the Messiahship of Jesus? How does this square with his doctrine of the Kingdom, and especially his great emphasis upon ethics? And may not the church have substituted a doctrine of Christ, his 'nature' or 'person', for Jesus' own teaching regarding the Kingdom of God and the way of gaining entrance to it by repentance, faith, and works of righteousness? Or must we conclude that the Gospel of the Kingdom was only one phase of Jesus' teaching, as the preaching of the Kingdom was perhaps only one phase of his mission; and that along with the message of the Kingdom went a claim to some personal prerogative—a claim perhaps originally secret, and made public only at the end of his career?

This is no doubt the impression conveyed by the gospels as a whole—not only by the Fourth Gospel, where the 'claims' of Jesus are advanced openly and unequivocally from the first, but even by the Synoptics, where he hints at the claim to Messiahship, but does not openly avow it until the scene in the house of the high priest. And yet, as we have seen, this is not the impression left upon us by a critical examination of the tradition underlying the gospels. Instead, the claim to Messiahship appears to be the reflection of the early church's belief in Jesus as the 'Coming One'.

Furthermore there is not one Christology in the gospels, there are several. And the most emphatic expressions of these Christological views are all but unquestionably the result either of editorial revision or of the reformulation of Jesus' sayings during the course of their oral transmission. As is well known, Mark's own Christology is of 'the Son of God' type—as in the title to his gospel (1:1), in the narratives of the Baptism and the Transfiguration (1:9-11; 9:2-8), in the summary description of Jesus' cures (3:9-12), and the words of the centurion at the cross (15:39). But the tradition of which Mark makes use contains a stratum, fairly distinguishable from the rest and characterized by the term 'the Son of Man', which has also been introduced into some of the sayings in the earlier

pericopes (e.g. in 2:10, 28). The proper point of departure for a consideration of this stratum is undoubtedly
the saying in the Little Apocalypse (13:26)—Mark's understanding of this term is uniformly (and properly)
determined by its apocalyptic usage, going back to Daniel
7:13. (The view that exceptions are to be found in chapter 2:10 and 28 is simply a device of modern exegesis.)
The same interpretation has influenced the tradition contained in Q,[13] the document (or cycle of stereotyped oral
tradition) which Matthew and Luke use in addition to
Mark.

It is not difficult to see what has taken place. The same
'editorial' treatment that characterizes Matthew's and even
Luke's substitution of the term for the first person sin-
gular (e.g. Matt. 16:13, Luke 6:22, 12:8) has been operative at the earlier level of the oral tradition. The term
reflects the belief and the hope of the primitive church,
not the thought nor the language of Jesus. What is difficult to see is how modern interpreters can assume that
Jesus thought of himself as the celestial 'Son of Man',
destined to come upon the clouds of heaven and hold the
last judgment; and at the same time attribute such deluded fanaticism to the perfectly sane, balanced, clear-
seeing and profoundly religious mind reflected in the main
body of the evangelic tradition. Perhaps an apologetic
value is thought to be found in such an assumed 'claim
of Christ', a kind of warrant for the (wholly reinter-
preted) Christology of the later creeds—along the line, no
doubt, of Father Tyrrell's defence of Catholic supernaturalism as primitive.[14] But at what cost! And with what
complete ignoring of the really crucial moment in primi-

tive Christianity, the resurrection and the experience of the Spirit, the visions of the risen Lord, and the most primitive faith of all, viz. that Jesus *became* Messiah at his victory over death. Orthodox Christianity does not really need to make this exegetical detour into ancient Jewish apocalyptic, following Schweitzer and the 'thorough-going eschatologists': the route is far more direct and far safer from the Prophet of Nazareth and his Gospel of the Kingdom to the creeds of Nicea and Chalcedon, to the faith and worship of the early Catholic church.

The New Testament lays emphasis upon the Messiahship of Jesus because that was the category in which the mystery of Jesus was set forth after the experience of his resurrection—no doubt inevitably, as *the only possible category, in the thought of the time,* in which it could be set forth. The gospels carry this back into the earthly life of Jesus, following Mark, whose major thesis is that Jesus was Son of God, or 'Son of Man',[15] even during his earthly ministry, and from the moment of his baptism; Matthew and Luke carry it back farther still, to his birth; John farthest of all—to his preëxistent state as the Logos or 'Word' of God.

But the claim to be Messiah was, we believe, never made by Jesus. Throughout its history, as Klausner has shown, that conception was thoroughly political; and Jesus never had the slightest intention of ascending a throne in Jerusalem. On the other hand the claim to be the celestial 'Son of Man'—a totally different idea from Messiahship—was not only foreign to Jesus' whole outlook but can be understood and maintained by his followers only by completely 'reinterpreting' the term—a process not undertaken even in the Passion Announcements of Mark. It was perhaps inevitable that Jesus should be so described in the early evangelic tradition; but that does not make it probable that Jesus himself used the term; moreover, as the church soon learned, the term was totally inadequate.

Jesus then was not 'the Son of Man coming on the clouds of heaven', but One who was—and is—vastly more significant, whose life and teaching, character and spirit, death and resurrection meant—and means—vastly more to the world than that quaint, archaic title could begin to convey. His real title, his real claim is far higher than this —as the church recognized when in its creeds and liturgies it effectually substituted other terms, though not discarding the old messianic terminology of the Parousia, the clouds of heaven, the judgment, and the resurrection of the flesh. This was the result of no fatal indulgence in Greek metaphysics: the old terms were inadequate, and better ones were required in which to set forth Jesus' uniqueness. Messiahship was not enough, and it failed to convey the most important thing of all, viz. the Christian faith in the adequacy and finality of Jesus' revelation of God. For out of all the countless millions who have lived on this earth he was the one person who saw things as they really are, and with the eyes of God, whose own life, character, and spirit were the perfect medium of the divine life, the divine character, the very 'Spirit' of God, and whose will was completely one with the will of God. The doctrine of the two natures in one person was only the ancient attempt to set forth this fact metaphysically and with all possible accuracy of definition; though the chief emphasis, let us not forget, lay upon ruling out false definitions (Gnostic and other) rather than upon the presumed finality of the definition set forth. The four classic terms of the Chalcedonian definition were all negatives: 'inseparably', 'unconfusedly', 'immutably', 'indivisibly'. It is a pity a fifth term was not added, viz. 'indefinably', or 'ineffably'. For there is real danger in thus attempting to define the indefinable; and we Christians should never forget that Christ is the object of *religious faith,* not of scientific knowledge—even of that science which we call theology. Christ can be worshipped only religiously; and the knowledge that we have of him is all but exclusively mediated by faith, and certainly not by the application of an aprioristic fifth-century metaphysics.

Contrasted with the Christ of the ancient creeds, how much less religious—to say the least!—is the conception popular in much New Testament exegesis during the past generation! The Jesus of 'thoroughgoing eschatology' is and remains a deluded fanatic, disguise it how we will, and simply ceases to command respect as a moral and religious leader. It is no use appealing to psychology and describing the 'absolute' consciousness of the religious genius. It does not cover the situation. Jesus is unique—but he is not mad. If he were mad, he would not be unique; indeed few institutions for the mentally deranged lack victims of the 'absolute' consciousness, who identify themselves with some great figure, past or present, natural or supernatural, or even with God. It is quite impossible that the downright sanity and health of mind reflected in the traditions of Jesus' life and teaching can be associated with one who either in his heart of hearts or openly and avowedly identified himself with the coming Judge of all mankind. Jesus' religion was 'healthy-minded', and he himself was no 'sick soul', to use the terms made classic by William James. There is a world of difference between Jesus and, say, Mohammed or the Mad Mullah or any one of dozens of fanatical military Messiahs the world has seen. The person who cannot recognize this difference has no business presuming to expound the gospels.

But it may be said, once more, that Jesus identified himself with the Suffering Servant of Second Isaiah and so, by combining this conception with the 'Son of Man' concept in Daniel, produced a wholly new idea of Messiahship. The combination is certainly new and unheard-of before the New Testament. But was it a conception of *Messiahship?* Jesus was unique; and 'Messiah' is after all—as a description of him—only an expedient, and a very inadequate one at that. Moreover, let us ask, which is the more probable: (1) that the early church, even the earliest church or some group within it, recognized the 'fulfilment' of the Servant prophecy in Jesus' sufferings, death, and resurrection, and so read the traditions of his life in its terms, combining it with that other early interpretation which recognized in him the coming Son of Man; or, on the other hand, (2) that Jesus identified himself with the Suffering Servant, and set out to realize the details of that picture, now understood as prediction? As we have already observed, there can be little question that the former is a more natural origin of the identification than the latter. Even if it is pointed out that Jesus consciously 'fulfilled' another prediction, viz. that of Zechariah (9:9), by riding into Jerusalem on an ass, as evidence that he thus purposely set about fulfilling prophecy, it will be recalled that it is not his disciples who are represented in the tradition as taking the initiative in greeting him as David or the Son of David, but the populace (the crowd of pilgrims; Mark 11:7-10; John 12:14); that even so he is still 'the prophet, Jesus, from Nazareth of Galilee' in the Matthean account (Matthew 21:10-11); while it is further noted even in the latest gospel, where presumably the tradition is most highly 'developed', that the disciples had no inkling at the time of any messianic demonstration, but only came to see this meaning in it at some later time (John 12:16). Under these circumstances, reflected in the tradition, it is impossible to believe that Jesus consciously set about fulfilling ancient prophecy!

Jesus is unique; and these attempted explanations go only part of the way in explaining him. They go less of the way now than ever before, since modern psychology has thrown a sharp light upon psychological types such as this explanation presupposes, and since the whole scheme of things presupposed in early Christian and first-century Jewish eschatology is all but inconceivable, as a serious theory of the world and of human destiny, to the present generation.

Nor is it necessary to assume some personal claim, messianic or other, to account for the death of Jesus at the hands of the Roman authorities. No such claim is required to account for the death of John the Baptist at the hands of Antipas. And it is extraordinarily significant that no messianic claim is advanced to account for Pilate's condemnation: Jesus is maligned by his enemies, but makes no statement in his own defence. Mark says frankly (15:19) it was for envy the chief priests delivered him up. The antagonism of the accredited teachers of the Law combined with that of the hierarchy in Jerusalem is entirely adequate to explain not only their demand for his execution but also Pilate's consent to their demand. The sole 'messianic' element was the charge of sedition: "He makes himself a king" and "prevents the collection of tribute, everywhere from Galilee to Jerusalem." But this charge is not only unsupported by any evidence, either at the trial before Pilate or elsewhere in the gospels as we now have them, but is preposterous on the face of it. Jesus was executed as John was—not as a rebel, not as a rival teacher hated by the scribes, not as a messianic claimant or pretender, but as the leader of a movement which was thought to be potentially dangerous. There were 'nerves' on both sides in that bitter time, and Pilate thought it safer a prophet with such a following as Jesus led should be permanently out of the way. It was hard enough to govern the Jews, without such leaders of religious movements stirring up the people—whatever their doctrines or their aims might be.[16]

Far then from Jesus' Gospel of the Kingdom setting an insoluble historical problem either from the standpoint of his own death at the hands of the Roman procurator or from that of the rise of New Testament Christology, it is indispensable for the explanation of both. (1) It was the misinterpretation of a widespread religious movement as political, perhaps by some of its friends and followers, certainly by its enemies, that made the crucifixion inevitable under the circumstances of the time. And it was the particular Jewish, theocratic, prophetic conception of the

Kingdom of God, as this-worldly though not political—in the ordinary sense of the word 'political'—that made the misinterpretation plausible. (2) It was the faith which Jesus aroused in his followers and their personal enthusiasm for him which convinced them that he was none other than the Agent of God in the establishment of his Kingdom. It was this faith and enthusiasm which not only explains their readiness for the resurrection experiences but made inevitable their interpretation of those experiences as proofs of Jesus' exaltation to heavenly Messiahship and the inauguration of the New Age soon to be crowned by his Parousia. The variety in the Christology of even the most primitive tradition makes it unlikely that one type and one alone goes back to Jesus: the inference must be that these were varieties in the primitive interpretation. For if Jesus had identified himself either with the Messiah, or with the Son of David, or with the Son of Man, for example, the other terms and conceptions could hardly have arisen among his earliest, closest followers.

The pivotal center alike of New Testament theology and New Testament history is the resurrection of Jesus. Until we recognize this fact we shall not adequately understand either Paul, the primitive pre-Pauline community, or the traditions embodied in the gospels. It was in the light of this great experience that the whole movement of early Christianity, from 'the beginning of the gospel' in the days of John to the anticipated Parousia of the Lord in the immediate future, that is to say its whole past and future, was interpreted by the New Testament church. But it was not viewed simply as an 'experience' on the

part of certain men: instead it was God's Act, God's
revelation, God's manifestation of his purpose in the whole
series of events seen in Jesus' ministry, teaching, death,
exaltation, and the outpouring of the Spirit. The center of
interest in the primitive community is of course different
from what it was in the lifetime of Jesus. But the ethics
of the Gospel, the ethics of the Kingdom, are no less important now than then. Otherwise how should they ever
have been preserved? But they are no longer ethics of the
Kingdom: they are now the mandates and commandments
of the Lord Jesus, which all must observe who would walk
in his 'Way' and obtain entrance into 'his' Kingdom when
it comes. The shift in interest is real. But the substance of
the ethics remains the same.

Now if all this is true, what are we to make of it in the
life, the teaching and activity of the church today? To
some persons it may seem that modern scholarship 'has
taken away the Lord, and we know not where they have
laid him'. To such persons modern scholarship may easily
become anathema—since its achievements seem purely de-
structive, perhaps even blasphemous. It calls for a totally
different conception of Jesus, they say, than that which
the church has upheld through the long centuries of the
past. As modern scholarship views the gospels, they no
longer set forth a pattern for the reconstruction of human
society, for the redeeming and sanctifying of human relationships. And we are really no better off now than we
were thirty years ago, when a tattered fragment of 'interim ethics' was offered us in place of the glorious gospel
of the saints and apostles of the Son of God!

This is a very negative view, and grossly exaggerated. I confess I cannot see that the situation has greatly altered, not only since three decades ago, but since a century—or even ten or twenty centuries—ago. As Paul insisted, the righteous man, the Christian, must live by faith. And that faith centers in the absolute and utter value of the *kind of life* Jesus lived and taught, rather than in some theological formula or hypothesis for explaining his nature or career. It is unfortunately quite possible to hold to the formula and deny the spirit, the real substance of Christian faith: like the man who insisted, "Of course I believe all that the creeds say about Jesus' divinity, but I don't think for a minute his teaching is practical!" That possibility of moral heresy, of ethical treason, is open to men today—but so it was in the first century. "Why call ye me Lord, Lord, and do not the things that I say?" (Luke 6:46). Christianity is not primarily a system of ideas, logically coherent and fitted each to the other in superb architectural unity. Christianity, certainly as the Gospel sets it forth, is a life, a spirit, a conviction, a faith. As a faith it uses all these various ideas and conceptions, which it inherited from Judaism or gathered up on its way through the Graeco-Roman world—uses them as terms in which to set forth what is really ineffable and beyond all human understanding. But it is still a faith, not the cheap substitute which Meredith described as

Unfaith clamoring to be coined to faith by proof.

May we still worship Christ, then? Certainly! Though we may or may not use the ancient terminology, or though we use it only with a historical interpretation, we can still worship Christ—provided only that for us the spirit of Jesus really is the revelation of God, and his way of life is for us the true way for men to live upon this earth as children of God and members of God's Kingdom. Any other worship of Christ is not heresy, nor even blasphemy, so much as it is utter insincerity, the 'lie in the soul' which as Plato said completely blinds a man and makes it impossible for him to tell right from wrong, truth from untruth, sincerity and devotion from hypocrisy and self-delusion.

But will the church rise to this new conception of faith, which is still the age-old conception set before us in the gospels? It must, if it is ever to open the eyes of this modern world to see the salvation of God, and to bring healing and peace to our distracted, disunited generation.

CHAPTER VIII

THE GOSPEL AND THE CHURCH

The point of view of this book has been historical rather than exegetical. Indeed, I have aimed to approach the central problem of the New Testament by the way of general history, first of all, rather than of the particular historical incidents recorded in the gospels or to be recovered by the exegesis of particular texts or passages. Both approaches are needed and, we may be confident, both are equally useful. Both have their limitations. If the danger of a purely historical approach is (reversing the popular proverb) to miss the trees for the wood, that of the purely exegetical approach is the exact opposite. Too often the exegetical approach has meant the reading-in of modern ideas (e.g. of medieval or later theological ideas) into the gospels. At least as a corrective the historical approach is greatly needed at the present time.

Christianity, we maintain, can accept this approach without hesitation: for Christianity, unlike some other religions, really takes history seriously. Equally in the New Testament as in the Old, the general course of human history and likewise its specific events, unrepeated and unrepeatable, are a revelation of the will, the purpose, the

character of God. This revelation of God in history cul-
minates in his final revelation of himself in Jesus Christ.
There is 'tension', 'antagonism', 'conflict', as the Barthians
say, though the meaning of the past is not exhausted in
this description. The central significance of the past is to be
seen, will eventually be made completely clear, in God's
victory over all that opposes him (II Thess. 2:4), his conquest of sin and death, his victory over evil—both in the
external universe and in the hearts and wills of men. The
biblical outlook is *telic,* or 'teleological', throughout. God
'sees the end from the beginning,' as any god, Greek or
pagan, must do; but the distinctive character of the God
of Israel—who is also the God of the New Testament, at
least of its earlier parts—is that he is the Living God, the
active, dominant force who 'will be what he will be'
(Exod. 3:14), who brings to pass that which lies outside
men's dim imaginings, and effects a salvation 'beyond
men's hopes and fears.'

The full meaning of God's purposes will be clear only
in the end. As any process is completely known only in
retrospect and from its final stage, so God's purposes will
be completely clear only when God has 'taken his great
power and reigns' over the whole world. Then at last the
mystery of God's past dealings with mankind, as Paul saw,
will be evident: 'for the Day will declare it'. And this
normal Christian view, certainly the one derived from the
scriptures of both Testaments, is anything but non-his-
torical, or anti-historical. History is the very fabric into
which the pattern of divine revelation has been woven—
a pattern to be seen not in ideas only, or in words, but
in deeds, in mighty acts. And the mightiest Act of God in

all history, according to Christianity—certainly according to the New Testament—is God's Act in Christ.

At last the long dim process has begun to take on meaning. It was God's purpose, evidently, not only through him to open up and to reveal a new way of salvation but to 'sum up all things in Christ' (Eph. 1:10), so that all God's ways with men, from the beginning, could now be understood in him. That is the whole point of the Logos doctrine. All God's revelation of himself, every 'word' since the first fiat of creation was like Christ's revelation of him, *was* Christ's revelation of him, continuous with it, identical with it. It is as if the author of the Fourth Gospel had boldly taken Paul's saying, 'We have the mind of Christ', and attributed it to God! God too has 'the mind of Christ'! That is, 'the spirit of life in Christ Jesus' is a spirit from God—in some true sense *is* God; and our access to the Father is not by some artificial way of cult or gift of hidden wisdom or secret device newly discovered by oriental priest or hierophant—as in Gnosticism or in the mysteries—but is direct, God having made himself known and accessible to us in the person of Jesus, in whom 'the Word became flesh and dwelt among us' (John 1:14).

The religion of the New Testament is jubilant and alive to its finger tips with the sheer glory of this experience. But it is no mystic trance men have fallen into—a few men, here and there, and then have told others about it. Instead, it is something multitudes have learned, something public and hence historical in the full sense; and it goes back historically to the fellowship men had with Jesus in Galilee, and still have with him as the risen, glorified, spiritual Lord and head of his church.[1]

Reading back from this experience, no title is adequate to convey their sense of his finality, authority, power. If he is 'now exalted at the right hand of God', as 'the Son of Man who is in heaven', he must have forseen his exaltation, and 'endured the cross, despising its shame', in order 'to enter into his glory'. If he is 'to come again with power and great glory', 'with all the angels of God', to hold the final judgment upon men and nations, then he must have foreseen and announced this—at least to his disciples. Even more, they too must have caught foregleams (at least once) of the glory that was eventually to be his; and so 'to chosen witnesses' on the mount he appeared 'wonderfully transfigured, in raiment white and glistering'.[2] If he was Messiah after death, by the power of his resurrection (this was the primitive *kerygma,* as Paul's quotation of it to the Roman Christians whom he had not yet visited makes clear), then surely he must have been Messiah before his death—certainly from the moment of his baptism; and the Gospel of Mark, as we now recognize, is the result of reading back the Messiahship of Jesus into his earthly life—an interpretation of the primitive tradition which was all but inevitable at the time and in the place where the Gospel of Mark was written. The later synoptists push the beginning of Jesus' Messiahship still further back, to the day of his birth or to the moment of his conception. John clears the way completely: there was never a moment, from the beginning of the world, when Christ the Word was not with God and, simply stated, *God.*[3]

Modern New Testament study now faces the question,

How valid is this interpretation?—granting that it is interpretation rather than record. Where must we draw the line between the early church's faith in Jesus' Messiahship—or rather in his exaltation, for which the only term then available was Messiahship—and the concrete actuality of Jesus' mission and message to his people? And if the interpretation appears to be a valid one, how adequate are the terms in which it is set forth—not only in the epistles and in the Apocalypse but also in the gospels? Did Jesus, or did he not, conceive himself to be God's Messiah, the pre-destined (or pre-designated) King of Israel? Or did he use some other term, e.g. 'Son of Man', or 'Son of God'; and if so, how are these terms distinguished from the title 'Messiah', i.e. 'the Lord's *Anointed*'? And if the primitive community doubtless looked upon him as the invisible head of the New Israel, soon to appear in glory, to what extent, if at all, did Jesus himself share this view, i.e. during the days of his earthly ministry?

In brief, how much of the language of the gospels is the language of devotion, of worship, of hymn and liturgy, of exhortation and warning addressed to the members of the New Israel in the thirties and forties and fifties, rather than the stenographic transcript or even the accurate oral account of what Jesus said, did, and purposed to do as he went about Palestine 'in the days of his flesh'? These are the questions, as we have seen, which the modern view of the gospels and particularly the view associated with 'Form Criticism' must face.

There is nothing in the New Testament that needs to be discarded, and there is a place for everything—even for

the variant readings of its manuscripts.[4] But we are trying
to gain a true historical perspective, and to see things
where they really belong: not an easy task, since the
sacred books of our religion were written, not as docu-
mentary records of a memorable religious movement, but
'from faith and to faith', and for the purpose of reënforc-
ing that faith. That faith, let us never forget, was not
faith in the credibility of certain records, but in a Person
actually present in the midst of the community of his
followers; no dead Pythagoras, the revered though de-
parted head of a school of philosophy, but a living Lord,
in the concrete specific sense of ancient Near Eastern
religion. That was the meaning of the term 'Lord', whether
in Greek ($\kappa\acute{v}\rho\iota os$) or in Aramaic (*Mar,* or *Maran:* 'our
Lord').[5] That the earliest Christians used such language
shows that the worship of Christ as divine dates from the
church's earliest period—long before our gospels, or even
the Pauline epistles, were written.

From the historical point of view, then, Jesus appears
as a Jewish teacher, and his doctrine of the Kingdom of
God is nothing new and revolutionary—not even in the
sense in which the doctrines of the apocalyptists were new
and revolutionary. If anyone thinks the Jewish apocalypses
(such as First Enoch, Jubilees, the Twelve Testaments,
the Assumption of Moses, Second Baruch, Second Enoch,
Fourth Ezra) throw all the light we need upon the teaching of Jesus, let him but read further and discover how
far apart are the views of the apocalyptists from his, how
vindictive and puerile, how narrow and partisan, how

crude and fantastic, how prejudiced and bitter are the minds that have produced those writings, how utterly unlike the mind and the spirit of Jesus of Nazareth.[6]

We incline to identify 'eschatological' and 'apocalyptic'; but the result is only confusion. *All* Hebrew-Jewish religious thought was 'eschatological', in the sense that it hoped great things from God, ventured great things for God, expected—and received—great things from God. All Hebrew thought slips readily from past to future, and back again—as the very tenses of its verbs make clear. But 'apocalyptic' means something else: the circle of bizarre, unwholesome, antisocial ideas cherished by those who cultivated strange visionary experiences, 'boldly walking about in things unseen', 'where angels fear to tread', and presuming to be the confidants of the Most High in all his plans and purposes for the future, down to the last detail. Of particular interest to them were the contrasting fates of the elect and the damned, and the intricate schedule of events in 'the time of the end'. And anyone who cannot distinguish between the outlook of these wild visionaries and that of Jesus of Nazareth must be hopeless indeed, both as a literary or historical critic and as an interpreter of religion. Jesus' teaching, as Easton and Goguel have rightly insisted, is 'eschatological but not apocalyptic'.

Jesus' eschatology is that of the prophets, now set forth under a new set of environing circumstances due to the altered situation of first-century Palestine. So too his ethics are the ethics of the Old Testament, restated in the highest, purest form. They presuppose the Old Testament, and cannot be taken in isolation from it.[7] And his doctrine of the Kingdom is likewise a Jewish doctrine: in fact it is only a succinct and inclusive term for the Reign of God anticipated by the prophets of the Old Testament and equally presupposed as the fundamental principle of religion in the Torah. God is the God of all the earth, the God of absolute justice or righteousness, who will save the righteous and punish the wicked; he is also the God of Israel, who chose to himself one particular people to be to him 'like a beloved and only son,' and Israel won merit in his sight by accepting at once the divine call to special privileges and special tasks, gladly taking upon itself 'the yoke of the Kingship of Yahweh' and responding, "We will keep all the words of this Law." The 'Kingdom' is simply the *Reign* of God, first over Israel, then over the whole world; yet this priority is not temporal, for God was the creator of the universe long before Adam was created or Abraham or Israel was born. And in Jesus' teaching, as in certain passages of the Old Testament, this primarily Jewish but essentially universal 'Kingdom' of God is to be 'opened to all believers' and many from the east and the west, the north and the south will 'sit down with Abraham, Isaac, and Jacob' at the banquet of the Age to Come (Matt. 8:11; Luke 13:29). It is the same universalism that we find in certain high points in older prophecy:

> In that day there will be a highway from Egypt to Assyria;
>   And the Assyrians will pass along it to Egypt,
>   And the Egyptians to Assyria;
> And the Egyptians will worship the Lord along with the
>   Assyrians.

In that day Israel will be a third with Egypt and Assyria, as a blessing in the midst of the earth, which the Lord of hosts has blessed, saying,

Blessed be Egypt my people,
And Assyria the work of my hands,
And Israel my inheritance!

(Isaiah 19:23-25)

The real test for entrance into the Kingdom or, as John the Baptist had proclaimed, the criterion at the coming judgment (Matt. 3:8-9), is not race or nationality or descent from Abraham but obedience to the Law of God the King. Indeed, this obedience was to transcend the limited sense in which the scribes were interpreting the Law. Though the gate was wide open to proselytes at that time and the Pharisees eagerly 'compassed sea and land to make one proselyte' (Matt. 23:15), Jesus' emphasis was laid upon the quality of the required obedience rather than upon the extension of Judaism as a religion, a cult, to the far corners of the earth. He conceived obedience to the Law of God in the fuller Old Testament sense of obedience in *spirit:* "Thou shalt love the Lord thy God with all thy heart . . . and thy neighbor as thyself: for this is the Law and the prophets" (Matt. 22:37-40). For all the fine things said by many a scribe and rabbi, their usual level of religious inspiration and insight was not really up to that of the Old Testament, as even the highest of Old Testament insights were not quite up to those of Jesus.

Jesus did not hesitate to criticize the limitations of scribal and Pharisaic interpretation of the Law; and he even went beyond criticism of their interpretation to criticism of the Law itself, as in his solution of the con-

flict between the permission of divorce and the intention
of the Creator revealed in the earlier passage in Genesis
(Mark 10:5-9). The principle is sound: law must be
interpreted in the light of its own clear intention, of the
lawgiver's purpose, expressed or implied. In this case the
intention of the divine lawgiver is clearly expressed. The
later permission of divorce (by Moses, vs. 5) can therefore be viewed only as a concession, a modification in
the actual enforcement of the law; and this meant an
evaluation, a criticism, of the Deuteronomic code as contrasted with the first book of Torah, Genesis. It is clear
then that, as Knopf, Branscomb, and others have said,
Jesus went beyond criticism of the current oral interpretation of the Law to criticize the Law itself.[8]

The Reign of God is coming, speedily and at once.
Indeed it is in a most real sense already here, and men must
decide (like Israel of old) whether they will respond and
obey or remain undecided, opposed or indifferent, and
so forego the benefits and blessings which it is already
bringing with it. The healing of the sick, the exorcism
of demons, the cleansing of the leprous, the restoration
of the dead, the good tidings proclaimed to the poor—all
these were 'signs' of the advent of God's Reign (Luke
4:17-21, 7:22, 9:2, 10:17-18; Matt. 10: 7-8). Though
no sign, of the portentous kind demanded by his contemporaries, should be given 'to this generation' (Mark
8:12)—to men too blind to observe 'the signs of the
times' (Matt. 16:3)—still Jesus and his followers, Jesus
and his mission were *the* sign God had given of his own
presence and power and of his purpose to establish now
at last his own direct and complete and perfect Reign

over the world. This was the thing 'greater than Jonah, or Solomon, or the temple' which was now 'here' (Matt. 12:6, 41, 42).

Like all the prophets, Jesus, as we saw, 'foreshortened the future', and viewed as immediate what was either vastly remote or even timeless. The immediate occasion of the 'New Prophecy' of John the Baptist was the threatening dangers that surrounded the nation. As in every time of crisis, from the days of the Philistine menace to Israel's independence in the eleventh century, and as in the days of Assyria's advance, and in that of the Neo-Babylonian and Persian empires, and again as in the days of Antiochus IV and the Seleucid tyranny, so once more the voice of prophecy bursts forth. Even the apocalyptic writings, so far as they retain contact with the great religious tradition of Israel, may be viewed as struggling efforts to find that voice and utter it afresh. And now, caught in a situation which was destined by another generation to 'blow up', as we say, in the cataclysm of the Jewish War, John and Jesus and the primitive apostles conveyed once more 'the word of the Lord' to a 'scattered and distracted people', warning and encouraging, threatening and reassuring, pointing out the one way of deliverance that God himself had provided—viz. repentance—and promising that before long God would take the reins of earthly power into his own hands and set up his Kingdom forever over all mankind.

What John did in announcing the Judgment, what Jesus did in announcing the Kingdom, the primitive Christians—including even Paul—did in describing the events which were to precede and accompany the final end. The whole New Testament, in various ways, reflects this 'eschatological' outlook—as do also the eschatological passages in the prophets, especially the 'happy endings' which either they or later editors have given their books.

Christianity, as a new religion, though at first a sect within the variegated fold of the ante-bellum Judaism of the first century, was in one sense a new synthesis of eschatological ideas. The *eschaton*, as Professor Dodd uses the term, was already present, had already arrived—at last was already in the process of arrival. It was like the transit of a celestial body, already begun, but destined to increase still more; or like a sunrise, 'that shineth more and more unto the perfect day'—with this difference, that the new day, the full meridian of the heavenly glory, once it comes, will be everlasting, world without end.

Thy Kingdom is an everlasting Kingdom,
And thy dominion endureth throughout all generations.
(Psalm 145:13)

This messianic dream, as we must call it from the purely historical point of view, died down by the end of the second century. Phrygian Montanism was its last flare-up. Origen and the Greek theology put out the last flickering embers, as far as 'the great church' was concerned—though various Christian groups have revived the hope from time to time. But there were signs of its weakening before the first century was out, or perhaps early in the second (Matt. 24:12). By the middle of the second century, doubt was vocal. "Where is the promise of his coming? For from the day that the fathers fell asleep all things

continue as they were from the beginning of the creation"
(II Peter 3:4).

What is its permanent value? Does it stand as a symbol
of the end of time, or of an eternal relation in which
men—and the whole world—stand to the will of God, i.e.
to his ultimate purposes in the creation of the universe
and of us, one species of his creatures? Is the eternal order
described in the Epistle to Hebrews and (less specifically)
in the Gospel of John the real order of things, the *only*
genuine and real order, and hence identical with the
'Kingdom' of God which is ever coming, yet never coming, but only exists evermore within the shadowy back-
grounds of man's fitful life upon this aging planet? Perhaps it stands for both. It is the Consummation, 'when
time shall be no more'; but it is also the eternal Reign of
God, from the beginning of the creation and forever. So
that, since Christianity is a religion, not a philosophy, the
eternal order can only be conceived as destined to 'come',
though it can 'come' only gradually, never completely,
within the time-series. Both ideas are closely related: for
only that can come to pass which has always been, and
always is, but now takes place in the immediate actuality
of God's specific purposes.

The thought of Jesus is clear, though modified and to
some extent distorted in later reflections, even in the New
Testament: God and his Reign are the one absolute, final
reality. And so instead of saying that God's Kingdom,
which is now unreal because unrealized and invisible, must
'come' and take the place of a real order, perhaps Satanic,
which now holds the field, it is far truer to say that God
reigns already, makes his sun to shine and his rain to fall

on evil and good alike, since "the Lord is loving unto every man, and his mercy is over all his works." What needs to be done is to remove all that now stands in the way of the fulfilment of his purposes. As the author of Matthew has phrased it, in thoroughly apocalyptic terms, "The Son of Man shall send forth his angels and they shall gather out of his Kingdom all things that cause stumbling, and them that do iniquity, and shall cast them into the furnace of fire" (Matthew 13:41).

Our earlier figure is still suggestive. A rebellious province must be conquered and reincorporated in the empire: man's rebellious will must be overcome; sin, disease, and death must be brought to an end; the demons must be curbed, banished, and destroyed; and all that contradicts and defies God in his world must be abolished—then and then only can come the end, the true *eschaton*, when God is 'all in all'. Paul's interpretation of Jesus' meaning is surely profounder than that of the early Christian apocalyptists—and the more significant in that Paul himself was not uninfluenced by them, especially perhaps in the earlier phase of his career.[9] And it was upon the basis of Jesus' own teaching, not that of Jewish or Christian apocalyptists, that the earliest doctrine of the church arose: the Church was the New, the True Israel, the Remnant, the authentic representative of the one and only *Qahal* or *Ecclesia* of God—through which alone, now, even the contemporary Israel could be saved by repentance and faith.

Following this summary of what we have been endeavoring to make clear in these lectures, we come now to a final question: What of the church today, weakened and disunited, threatened by its foes and undermined by widespread indifference? There are those who talk glibly of 'the twilight of Christianity'—but they also talk about 'the twilight of the gods', and seem to assume that all religion is on the wane. Is this probable? For twenty-five *thousand* years, perhaps, certainly for ten thousand, since the end of the Late Stone Age, men have been more or less religious, and have let their faiths fade into the twilight only to find brighter and more inspiring ones on the morrow. Religious decline and revival have been quite as characteristic of social history as have been the decline and rise of civilization, of art, of letters, of thought. So we need not lose hope. Ours is not a very religious age—we are too much occupied in 'finding out many inventions' to pay adequate regard to things no man ever invented but are old as the stars and the hills, indeed older. But a day will surely come, if history follows any pattern or teaches any lesson, when faith will come surging back in a fresh tide and man's goings will once more be ordered by the will of One greater than man, even his Creator. And so we are not discouraged, not even by the revolt of half of Europe against the church, or even by the desperate and extremely dangerous disunity of the church itself. Whatever happens to the church, God's Kingdom is from everlasting to everlasting—God reigns supreme. Hence we believe the revolt in Europe will subside; that out of it, somehow, will come a purer, stronger Christian faith; and we welcome the signs of a growing unity in the church, at least outside the continent of Europe, and especially in our own English-speaking world.

We are equally confident in the future of 'liberalism' in Christianity, that is of the principle of intellectual freedom, with an open Bible and a stronger emphasis upon ethics than upon dogma. If, as I believe, these principles are to be identified with Christian 'liberalism,' then we may say we have confidence in its future. For all the harsh words spoken against it, and all the bitter adjectives—'shallow, insincere, obtuse, self-satisfied, complacent, bourgeois', and, climax of all, 'bankrupt'!— we still believe in it and in its future. For modern 'liberalism' is really the continuation of a tradition at least three hundred years old in the English-speaking world, and has, we believe, a future at least as long as its past—that is until its task has been fully accomplished. Some of its harshest critics, it may be suspected, either know too little of history to understand the present, or else are too unaware of the real issues in the present to have any genuine interest in the past. And some, we fear, look upon our world only through the haze that hangs over the ancient but still contested battle fields of central Europe. America, the stronghold of present-day religious liberalism, either has no theology, on this version, or else merely imports a diluted brand from abroad. We Americans are 'activists', forsooth, our universities more interested in football than in metaphysics, our churches more concerned over social service than over theology or worship or the deep things of the spiritual life. The charge is much too true, alas! —though one cannot help wondering if the tragic chaos of the world might perhaps have been averted if the social gospel had been adequately preached—and applied—in central Europe during the past forty years.

Nevertheless we must admit that the charge against us is true. We really are too much busied with things, with movements, programs, activities. And yet, for all our obsession with activity, there is growing up today a virile American theology which eventually, if Europe ever comes to its senses and recovers from the war-fever that has cursed its peoples for countless generations, may have something to offer toward the reconstruction of religious thought upon some better basis than the already antiquated formulae of 'tension', 'crisis', 'super-historical', 'dialectic', and all the absurd lingo of theological nihilism. It is this new emphasis in theology, with its background of political and social liberalism; with its genuine and serious interest in history; with its great central theistic emphasis, i.e. upon God and the Reign of God, rather than upon the pathological elements in human experience; with its greater concern over the essential Gospel of Jesus than over the divergent later interpretations of that Gospel, some of which are to be found even in the New Testament—it is this characteristic emphasis in American theology which gives us renewed hope, and provides an answer to the criticisms of our religion made by those whose peculiar and unfortunate experience in a world incessantly at war in large measure prevents their understanding the American outlook.

The Kingdom of God has been identified time and again with specific institutions, from the Catholic church of the second century to the Holy Roman Empire, and then on to the Second German Reich and the British Empire under the great and good Victoria. I do not intend to close these lectures by identifying it with American democracy, or with any existing institution or state! Nevertheless, the American dream of a new way of life for man upon this earth, in a world at peace, where justice is achieved and maintained between nations, groups, and individuals, with liberty for all and a fair chance for every child of man to realize to the full his God-given talents and capacities—surely that dream, though too often denied in actual practice, is 'not far from the Kingdom of God'. *Under the conditions and circumstances of our modern world,* something like that is the only possible expression of the hope of the Kingdom, that is of the actual Reign of God over his world.

No purely other-worldly kingdom, whether within the quiet recesses of the inner spirit of the individual or beyond the confines of time in a remote hereafter, can be an adequate equivalent to Jesus' doctrine of the Kingdom of God. Nor is the church, as an empiric institution, identical with the Kingdom, but only the church in its ideal aspect, in the light of that goal toward which it must ever strive and aspire. Only so may the church be described as the Kingdom of God. Its divorce from the state, as here in America, does not in itself make it any the more 'spiritual', any more truly the Kingdom of God. Though divorced from the state, and properly so, its concern must be no less the welfare of the nation, the welfare, that is, of the people who make up the nation. As Canon Barry has remarked, the work of the church *ought* to be largely 'secular'.[10] It exists to serve society and individuals, to mediate divine grace, to build a stronger unity of fellowship within the political unity of the state—and beyond the state, within the whole human race conceived as a unity. As the Catholic theologians frankly recognize, Christianity is in its very essence super-national, and can no more stop short of the whole *orbis terrarum* than can communism—even less so. It must embrace the whole world, eventually, or perish in the attempt. Hence Christian 'missions' is no afterthought, but is one with the basic urge which brought Christianity into existence. As with missions, so with education, public health, law and order, justice in industry, everything in short that is embraced within the welfare of human beings, down to such details as soil-conservation and the reforestation of now arid areas. Kagawa sees it clearly enough! Nothing human is really alien to the Kingdom of God! Far from shaming us, the charge of 'activism' is one we may well rejoice in, one we may hope even more fully to deserve!

How then can we *preach* the Gospel of the Kingdom, these days? In the first place, the eschatological emphasis is certainly lacking in modern Christianity—except for those who live under a threat similar to that which first produced it in ancient Israel, and for those who share by sympathy in this outlook. But there is no use in trying to revive it artificially for the rest of us. The tragedy of war is close enough to bring it home to men everywhere in the world, today. More than that, each one of us faces the prospect of death: the *certainty* that before many years, at most, we shall have left this scene of action for, we trust, some other; the *possibility* that any day may be our last. Yet this is hardly the equivalent of the outlook of the early Christians. Be it so; there is no use in trying to revive that outlook artificially. Eschatology will probably continue inevitably to be a minor emphasis in our teaching—as it has been for the church as a whole since the second century.

But in the next place, the emphasis upon the transcendence of God, the sovereignty of his will, the reality of his purposes, his wisdom, his justice—quite as much as upon his love—all this needs greater emphasis today. Without it, the Gospel of the Kingdom is utterly incomprehensible—whether in its ancient biblical form or in its modern theological or even sociological interpretation. Upon the basis of a *practical* humanism, whatever our theology, it is inconceivable that the Christian religion can continue indefinitely to hold the allegiance of men. There are multitudes today who apparently have not the faintest conception of God or experience of him. Wisely the Anglican bishops assembled at Lambeth ten years ago called upon all Christians everywhere, especially the clergy in their teaching and preaching, to lay more emphasis upon the doctrine of God. Here then is one item of primary importance which should go into our preaching of the Gospel of the Kingdom.

Thirdly, some of us had hoped that the bishops might in 1940 issue another call to the Christian world, and bid us all study and teach and preach the doctrine of the Kingdom. The Lambeth Conference will not be held, on account of the war. But there is no reason why we who feel its importance should not go ahead so to study and teach.

Men sometimes say that the church has no program, that its ideals are all aloft and floating in the air, without even ground ropes for bringing them down to earth.

"Communism", they say, "ah, there is a program!" Yes, a program—if a definite program is all that is required, regardless of its underlying theory or practical consequences!

To be specific, what would a Christian society be like?— I mean one in which the principles of Jesus' Gospel of the Reign of God should be fully carried out and practiced. This is where we Christians must put our minds at work and think in terms of modern social, economic, political, educational science and policy. The danger is that we may identify some one program of welfare—e.g. the prohibition of the liquor trade—with the total interests of the Kingdom of God. But we must take that risk, and then try to avoid the danger. To refuse to think concretely about the actual situation and the actual goal toward which we should strive is only wasting time and getting us nowhere. True, there is also, on an even wider scale, the recurrent danger of Christian legalism, which assumes that our Lord's Gospel can somehow be articulated in a code, with rules governing every aspect of human behavior or at least every possible application of the 'new law' to the conditions and circumstances of human life. But, as always, there is an opposite danger: either the casuists, the moral theologians, the experts in ethics, historical and philosophical, will be asked to deal scientifically and to the best of their insight with the concrete problems of conscience, or else Mrs. Grundy will decide what is and is not 'proper' or 'Christian' or 'right'—with a consequent chaos in moral ideals, and confusion worse confounded in the teaching of the young, who naturally revolt, but revolt sometimes against things that are sane and wholesome as well as against those whose only authority is the stuffy, smug propriety of amateur moralists or the old-fashioned prejudices of the adult generation.

For example, pure legalism pervades much of the current discussion of divorce and remarriage, and our Lord's teaching is quoted as if it were a law. Strangely enough, this is the only law so cited from the Gospel, as if his equally trenchant saying about oaths were not likewise then a law; strangely too, since it makes the Christian faith a religion with one and only one binding law, that forbidding remarriage after divorce! The whole subject needs a fresh approach. The modern status of women, thanks to nineteenth-century Feminism and to woman's equality of rights at law, has considerably altered the bearing not only of canon law but of the gospel teaching whose literal interpretation resulted in the church's regulations. The truly Christian solution of the problem of divorce is certainly not along the lines of a crude, rule-of-thumb application of canon law, sometimes creating as many problems as it solves; or of the literal interpretation of a saying in the gospel which referred to an entirely different situation; instead, it must move in the direction of applying the *spirit* of Jesus to all the problems of family life. And here such factors as health, physical and mental, economic status, social security, education, temperament and interests—all these and still other factors must be taken into account; and the solution must be somewhat more consonant with the spirit of the Gospel than has been the solution common throughout large areas of the church in the past—more notably, perhaps, in the Anglican church than in the Roman or the Protestant churches, certainly more so than in the Eastern churches.

Or take another example, the doctrine of property. Does it necessarily follow from the Gospel that the old, biblical, ancestral, indeed primitive equation, piety equals poverty—readily convertible into that other, poverty equals piety—is good at all times and in all circumstances? It was true enough, no doubt, in a society like that of the 'pious and humble', the 'pious poor' of ancient Palestine, where men voluntarily renounced opulence abroad in order to live within the church-state community of the second commonwealth in the holy land; where a godly minority faced the constant threat of oppression and persecution, and where even God seemed to make men's lives hard, with recurrent famine and the unavoidable dangers of war to which Syria and Palestine had always been exposed. But in a responsible modern democratic society, with ample resources, and no danger of invasion across indefensible frontiers, the situation is utterly different! But here again the *spirit* of the Gospel is as imperative and as illuminating as ever. Wealth is not an end in itself; to make it such is to frustrate and stultify the very souls of those who thus mistake the purpose of their existence. Wealth may only be held in trust, in stewardship; and the ways in which it is obtained and held and expended or administered are all equally matters of deep social concern. Here the church should take the lead—in careful thought and study as well as in bold open pronouncement: hard thinking *first*, before hard preaching!

For there are certainly factors involved here that cannot be solved by a thirty-minute discussion group, hastily going over the data and then setting forth their findings in a series of drastic resolutions. For example, there is probably no hope of either social security for the individual or of social solidarity for the community unless something is done at both extremes of our present economic system. On one hand there is far too great a gap between the rich and the poor—no society can be healthy where this unbridged gulf exists. Moreover, under present conditions the greatest rewards too often go to those whose only claim is cleverness, whose only effective motive is selfishness, rather than to those whose creative capacity, skill and performance have contributed either to the wealth or to the welfare of society. The clever manipulator of other men's labor or possessions amasses a fortune; but the doctor whose skill saves his life and preserves him in health, the teacher who educates his children, the farmer who feeds him—these are often paid less than the domestics who serve the rich man's table. Meanwhile, the toiling—or unemployed—millions who create the wealth thus manipulated live at levels below that of normal subsistence. No society can stand that sort of thing indefinitely!

At the other extreme are those who persist in bringing into the world children whom they cannot feed, clothe, or prepare for life either by education or even by adequate physical care in infancy and childhood. Too many of these are low-grade in quality, physically, mentally, and morally, and are not a fit contribution to American life. We hear much discussion of the crime of wealth in the church; not so much about the crime of contaminating the nation's blood-stream. But one is equally as important as the other; and if one is a proper subject for the pulpit and for the discussion group, why not the other?

We do not hesitate to discuss poverty and unemployment, sometimes freely accusing certain classes or groups with responsibility for the present situation. But how can we conscientiously deal with these problems and leave out factors which are absolutely fundamental to their solution? Experts assure us that there is simply no hope of a permanent cure of the evils of poverty and unemployment unless this endless social liability is checked. Yet we preachers go on discussing them without ever mentioning this, the really fundamental problem. Here again the church must do some hard thinking—hard thinking *first*, before hard preaching.

These are examples of real issues before the church and especially its pulpit, and they should give us very great concern—that is, if the church really belongs in the heart of things, and takes the Gospel of the Reign of God upon earth in thorough earnest. How much less important and less urgent, relatively, are the appeals we often hear—to repent of the sin by which we helped bring on the European war, for example: a purely artificial appeal if ever there was one! We know perfectly well we did not bring on the European war, and it gives us no added confidence in preachers to hear that appeal from the pulpit.

Or take our endless academic discussion of pacifism as another example. It is presented as if the Gospel of Christ were purely pacifist, and men could sit by and watch their homes bombed, their children maimed and blinded, and make no resistance! When resistance is perfectly futile, as in first century Palestine, there is nothing else to do: the superb realism of Jesus stands out clearly in his recognition of this fact. But one need not hate an enemy, private or public—that is a different matter! And here again the majesty of his spirit overtowers our circuitous little beaten paths of thought. Non-resistance under persecution, non-resistance of national enemies when the odds are absolutely against you, non-resentment of persecutors and enemies alike—there is a Gospel which we have scarcely begun to comprehend, let alone take in full earnest. But it lies miles on the other side of modern 'pacifism' with its fatal principle of irresponsibility. Let pacifists, and especially those of us who preach, take in full earnest the causes that underlie war: materialism, self-centered nationalism and racialism, territorial aggression, the seizure and exploitation of weaker nations and of the earth's natural resources. That is where the burden of our prophecy should begin: repentance and a new attitude on these questions!

These are only a few points upon which the interpretation and the application of the Gospel of the Kingdom of God require careful thought, and then clear presentation in the pulpit, in the church school, in the discussion-group, and wherever men meet to talk over things that matter most. When it comes to the ethics of the Gospel, and of the Christian religion, we have a task on our hands these days, here in our hard-headed, 'practical', realistic America, that promises to take all we have of knowledge, skill, and devotion. But, in the words of Plato, "The prize is goodly, and the hope of winning it is great".[11] All the greater is it that the 'prize' is nothing less than a clearer understanding and a further extension of the Kingdom, the Reign of him to whom we pray:

> *Our Father, hallowed be thy name:*
> *Thy Kingdom come,*
> *Thy will be done*
> *On earth as it is in heaven.*

NOTES AND REFERENCES

CHAPTER I

The Jesus of History

1. See J. Jackson's note in the *Loeb* Tacitus, iv. 278.

2. These details—the tower, the costume, and the harp—are supplied by other writers, not by Tacitus, who says only, "Rumor had it that he mounted his private stage and . . . sang the destruction of Troy."

3. For the use of κωλύω as 'prevent', see I Esd. 6:6, Sir. 4:23, 46:7, I Macc. 13:49, III Macc. 1:13, 3:2, IV Macc. 14:16-17, etc. See Hatch and Redpath, *Concordance*, s.v.

4. That Galilee paid tribute to the tetrarch and not to the emperor is evident from Josephus's statement that when Antipas was banished his 'money' was given to Agrippa (*Ant.* xviii. 7.2 = § 252). Apparently the income was impounded during his absence, as was that of Herod the Great upon his death, and that of Archelaus upon his banishment (xvii. 9.3 = § 221; 13.2 = § 344). Even though Antipas was banished his funds were not seized by the emperor. In xvii. 11.4 = § 318-320, Josephus says explicitly that Galilee and Perea paid annual tribute of 200 talents to Antipas, while Philip's territory paid him but 100. Even after the drastic reduction of taxation by one fourth and the exemption of certain cities (by order of Caesar) and the separation of others which were added to the Province of Syria, Archelaus received a tribute of 600 talents a year from Judea,

Idumea, and Samaria. (Incidentally this shows the relative prosperity of Galilee and the south!)

5. Victor E. Harlow, *Jesus' Jerusalem Expedition*, Oklahoma City, 1936.

Chapter II

The Tradition Behind the Gospels

1. See my article, 'The Significance of Divergence and Growth in the New Testament', in *Christendom* iv. 4 (1939), pp. 575-587.

2. For the significance of the symbols Q, L, M, see any modern Introduction to the New Testament or to the Synoptic Gospels, for example B. H. Streeter, *The Four Gospels*, 1924, rev. ed. 1930, or my much briefer *The Growth of the Gospels*, 1933, or the more recent *Origins of the Gospels*, by F. V. Filson, 1938, esp. ch. v.

3. See the great work of H. M. and N. K. Chadwick, *The Growth of Literature*; it is still in course of publication: Vol. I, 1932, Vol. II, 1936, Vol. III, promised for 1940.

4. For an introduction, see H. L. Strack, *Introduction to the Talmud and Midrash*, Eng. tr., Philadelphia, 1931.

5. For an introduction, see A. Guillaume, *The Traditions of Islam*, Oxford, 1924.

6. For an introduction, see J. A. Bewer, *The Literature of the Old Testament in its Historical Development*, New York, 1922; or J. Hempel, *Die Althebräische Literatur*, Potsdam, 1930 (beautifully illustrated).

7. See the bibliography in Rauschen's *Patrologie* (new ed. by B. Altaner), Freiburg, 1931, § 45.

8. For an introduction, see G. Murray, *The Rise of the Greek Epic*, 2d ed., Oxford, 1911.

9. See my *Growth of the Gospels*, 1933, pp. 176-199. A late date is supported also by Bacon, Enslin, McNeile, Smith, Stanton, and others.

10. See Strack, *Introduction to the Talmud and Midrash*, p. 4.

11. See e.g. the Introduction to B. H. Branscomb's volume on Mark in *The Moffatt New Testament Commentary*, 1937; D. W. Riddle, *The Gospels, Their Origin and Growth*, 1939, esp. ch. vii.

12. Form Criticism may be applied to the Book of Acts as well as to the gospels: see the article by Professor Sherman Johnson, 'A Proposed Form-Critical Treatment of Acts' in *Anglican Theological Review*, xxi. 1 (Jan. 1939) pp. 22-31. Moreover tradition underlies more than one passage in the New Testament epistles, not only the obvious accounts of the Resurrection (i.e. the list of appearances of the risen Lord) and the Last Supper (the narrative) in Paul but also the more didactic portions of later epistles. See Philip Carrington, *The Primitive Christian Catechism* (Cambridge Univ. Press, 1940).

CHAPTER III

'The Beginning of the Gospel': John the Baptizer

1. So the Latin manuscripts, Codex Bezae, and others.

2. There are undoubtedly later touches in these verses. 'The time is fulfilled' is Pauline (cf. Gal. 4:4); on the contrary the evangelic tradition elsewhere represents Jesus as repudiating the apocalyptic reckoning of times and seasons (Mark 13:32; cf. Acts 1:7, though see Luke 21:24). The 'fulfilment' may of course not imply any such elaborate schemes as those suggested in Daniel, IV Ezra, II Baruch, etc. 'Believe in the gospel' also sounds Pauline or editorial. Matthew's simpler formulation is perhaps to be preferred: "From that time Jesus began

to preach and to say, Repent ye, for the Kingdom of heaven is at hand" (Matt. 4:17).

3. Probably not Perea, which was as much under Herod Antipas's control as was Galilee.

4. The Fourth Gospel even represents Jesus as leading a rival baptismal movement to that of John (3:22-23; 4:1), even before John was imprisoned (3:24). On this, see B. W. Bacon, *The Gospel of the Hellenists*, 1933, chh. x and xvi.

According to Matthew, on the other hand, Jesus withdrew to Galilee when he *heard* that John had been delivered up, and leaving Nazareth came and lived in Capernaum. "From that time he began to preach." Where he had been before returning to Galilee is not said; the Temptation Narrative alone occupies the interval between his baptism and return; and an interval is certainly suggested between his return to Galilee and his removal to Capernaum and the beginning of his preaching. See M. Goguel, *Life of Jesus*, Eng. tr. 1933, ch. viii; see also his *Jean-Baptiste: au Seuil de l'Évangile*, 1928; K. L. Schmidt, *Der Rahmen der Geschichte Jesu*, 1919, pp. 32-38.

5. John's explicit statement (3:22) is corrected later (4:2).

6. See Professor R. Bultmann's new commentary in the Meyer series.

7. See J. Weiss, *The History of Primitive Christianity*, Eng. tr. 1937, i. 9.

8. Especially ch. vii.

9. Probably, as Matt. 23:34-39 suggests, a continuation of the Wisdom oracle quoted in Luke 11:49-51.

10. Not only of the Synoptics with John, but of Luke's 'Longer Insertion' (9:51-18:14) with the statement in Mark 10:1.

11. Mark 4:11-12 is an 'editorial' interpretation of the tradition which the very parables given in the remainder of the chapter sufficiently refute.

12. See my paper, 'The Gospel in the New Testament' in *The Gospel and the Predicament of Modern Man* (Church Congress, 1939), pp. 10-24.

13. Professor Moffatt has advanced the view (in *The History of Christianity in the Light of Modern Knowledge*, Harcourt, 1929, pp. 187f) that John's message was: "I have baptized you with water, but he shall baptize with *fire*," the insertion of 'holy Spirit and' being due to later Christian reformulation. This would account for John's followers' later ignorance of the holy Spirit (Acts 18:24-19:7).

14. See K. Marti in Bertholet's edition of Kautzsch, *Die Heilige Schrift des Alten Testaments*, 1923, ii. 112, on the concluding verses of Malachi; B. Duhm, *Israels Propheten*, 1916, p. 360; Fleming James, *The Personalities of the Old Testament*, 1939, p. 421.

15. See J. Montgomery, *The Samaritans*, 1907, pp. 239ff; W. Bousset, *Die Religion des Judentums*, new ed., 1926, pp. 224f.

16. That idea belongs to a wholly different circle of eschatological ideas, but since it was so strongly repudiated we can only assume that later Christians or 'Baptists' must have taken it for granted; cf. Luke 3:15, John 1:20.

17. And in the gloss from Matthew in vs. 6, taken almost word for word from the description of John in the LXX. See my article, 'Studies in the Text of St. Mark' in the *Anglican Theological Review*, xx. 2 (Apr. 1938) pp. 103-119; L. Vaganay, *Initiation à la Critique Textuelle Néotestamentaire*, 1934, pp. 166ff.

18. As against the 'mythological' view which would take the 'one like unto a son of man' in Daniel 7:13 as a personal being, see Professor Montgomery's note in his Commentary on Daniel (*International Critical Commentary*), 1927, pp. 317-324.

19. See also Ezek. 36:25; and note in Strack-Billerbeck, *Kommentar z. N.T.*, i. 112f.

20. Johannes Weiss, *Die Predigt Jesu vom Reiche Gottes*, 2d ed., Göttingen, 1900, p. 67.

CHAPTER IV

The Public Career of Jesus

1. For this interpretation, viz. that the first half of the verse is a quotation of some current estimate of John, perhaps identifying him with some messianic figure, see R. Bultmann, *Die Geschichte der synoptischen Tradition*, 2d ed., 1931, p. 178. See also the essay by E. W. Parsons, 'John the Baptist and Jesus', in *Studies in Early Christianity*, ed. by S. J. Case, 1928; also his more recent one, 'The Significance of John the Baptist for the Beginnings of Christianity' in the *'Case-Festschrift'* entitled, *Environmental Factors in Christian History*, ed. by J. T. McNeill, M. Spinka, and H. R. Willoughby, Chicago, 1939.

2. O. Holtzmann, *The Life of Jesus*, Eng. tr., 1904, pp. 400-401.

3. In his posthumous book, *Der Messias*, ed. by Hans Schmidt, Göttingen, 1929.

4. See Carl H. Kraeling, *Anthropos and Son of Man*, 1927; Ed. Meyer, *Ursprung und Anfänge des Christentums*, 1921, ii. 345-352.

5. So M. S. Enslin, in *Quantulacumque*, 1937, pp. 117-122, 'The Date of Peter's Confession'. See also Lohmeyer's long note, in his Commentary on Mark, 1937, pp. 178-181.

6. Though Perea was certainly under the jurisdiction of Herod Antipas (see above); on this view Jesus evidently remained in Galilean territory until the last stage of his journey.

7. But we must assume, I believe, that the demonstration was a spontaneous one on the part of the disciples, not one planned by Jesus himself (see p. 72). The Gospel of John says explicitly that the disciples did not at the time grasp the full significance of the event, 'but after Jesus was glorified they remembered that this was said of him in scripture and that it had happened to him' (12:16 Goodspeed).

8. Despite the able argument of J. Jeremias, *Die Abendmahls-worte Jesu*, Göttingen, 1935. See Professor Easton's review in the *Anglican Theological Review* xvii (1935), pp. 173f.

9. The passage in Mark 14:61b-64 is thought by some to be a secondary element in the tradition—the last of the Son of Man sayings, the climax of them all, and the key to all. Its omission leaves a lacuna in the narrative, and alters the whole perspective of the life of Jesus; but this is scarcely an adequate reason for assuming that the verses are *literatim et verbatim* a record of the final stage of the proceedings before the high priest.

10. See Chapter VI, note 9.

11. See J. Weiss, *The History of Primitive Christianity*, i. 23-31, 83-104. The very term used, ὤφθη, is the technical term for 'appearance in vision', 'manifestation', in the Greek Old Testament and elsewhere; cf. Gen. 12:7, 17:1 (LXX).

12. As I have noted elsewhere Johannes Weiss held this to be a translation of the primitive Christian (Aramaic) title, 'Son of Man'. See his Commentary on I Cor. 15:47. But was not the 'Son of Man' identical with the Messiah? There lies the crux of interpretation! Though frequently taken for granted at the present day, the identification is far from certain. Only two passages in I Enoch support it, 48:10 and 52:4. In the first of these two passages (where Charles's note needs to be brought up to date) it may be suspected that the text has gone astray or been interpolated, and should read:

For they have denied <the name of> the Lord of Spirits

(*omitting* 'and His Anointed'). Thus it would conform to 41:2, 45:2, 46:7. The second passage does not really refer to the Son of Man at all, but to the earthly kingship, as in Psalm 72; it occurs in the section devoted to 'the Elect One'. The two figures, Son of Man and Elect One, are characteristic of two distinct strands (or sources) in the book; see Charles's translation, 1912 edition, p. 65.

13. Accurately summarized in Goguel's *Life of Jesus*, Eng. tr. 1933, ch. iii, 'The Pauline Evidence'.

14. *The Present Task in New Testament Studies,* 1936; see pp. 35-41.

15. That is, of the Palestinian communities; the tradition in Gentile communities was of course derivative, as e.g. in Mark, 'the Roman gospel'.

CHAPTER V

The Background of Jesus' Message

1. Stephen Liberty, *The Political Relations of Christ's Ministry,* Oxford, 1916.

2. See B. W. Bacon, *Studies in Matthew,* 1930; E. Lohmeyer, *Galiläa und Jerusalem,* 1936, and Commentary on Mark in the Meyer series, 1937; R. H. Lightfoot, *History and Interpretation in the Gospels,* 1934, *Locality and Doctrine in the Gospels,* 1938.

3. So F. C. Burkitt, e.g. in *Christian Beginnings,* 1924; see pp. 84, 89.

4. M. Holleaux, in *Cambridge Ancient History,* viii. 223, prefers the year 189, but only because he believes the battle was fought in January.

5. Technically 27 B.C., when he became *Princeps.* M. Rostovtzeff, *A History of the Ancient World,* ii. 178.

6. See H. St. John Thackeray, *Josephus the Man and the Historian,* 1929, p. 69.

7. Of course, unfortunately, large parts of the *Annals* are missing at points of great relevance to Jewish (and early Christian) history: part of Books v and vi, all of vii-x and part of xi, part of xvi and all of xvii-xviii. These covered such important years as 29-31, 37-47, 66 and following. Moreover his *Histories* is broken off before we get to the capture of Jerusalem by Titus in the year 70.

8. For example the 'Little Apocalypse' in Mark 13 (verses 7-

8, 14-20, 24-27), the substratum of which can perhaps be dated in 40-41; it was occasioned by Caligula's attempt to have his statue placed in the temple in Jerusalem.

9. Commagene became part of the Province of Syria in 18 A.D. Tacitus, *Annals* ii. 56. Cf. Pauly-Wissowa-Kroll, *Suppl.* iv. 984.

10. See *Antiquities* xvi. 1-5 for Herod's 'innovations' in 'changing the laws'.

11. See my *Economic Background of the Gospels*, 1926, Part ii, 'The Economic Data'.

12. The only way the ancient world knew of solving problems of over-population or under-production was conquest. There are nations in the modern world which have not advanced beyond that solution.

13. See my *Economic Background of the Gospels*, p. 89.

CHAPTER VI

The Gospel of the Kingdom

1. In Sotah 9:15, probably an interpolation.

2. This seems a more probable explanation than that the Christian church took over apocalyptic and hence Judaism was compelled to abandon its use for apologetic purposes.

3. See e.g. IV Ezra 9:26, 12:51; Mart. Isa. 2:11.

4. See J. Montgomery, 'Ascetic Strains in Early Judaism', in the *Journal of Biblical Literature*, li. 3 (1932), pp. 183-213.

5. Cf. J. Héring, *Le Royaume de Dieu et sa Venue*, 1937, ch. i.

6. Meg. 31a; cf. Singer's *Jewish Prayer Book*, pp. 214f., 'Rabbi Jochanan said . . ." C. G. Montefiore and H. Loewe, *A Rabbinic Anthology*, 1938, pp. 30, 474.

7. Barn. 16:9, II Clem. 6:7; cf. J. Weiss, *The History of Primitive Christianity*, i. 77-82, ii. 554ff.

8. As in certain passages in the Apostolic Fathers, e.g. II Clement 17:5, "The unbelievers . . . will be amazed when they see the kingdom of the world given to Jesus"—i.e. at the end of the age (contrast I Cor. 15:24-25). The term used here is τὸ βασίλειον, 'dominion over the cosmos', not the familiar βασιλεία of the gospels.

9. As was proposed, according to the apocryphal *Gospel of Nicodemus* 4:3; compare the Talmudic legends of Ben Stada and Jeshu ha-Notzri (Sanh. 67a, 43a). See R. T. Herford, *Christianity in Talmud and Midrash,* 1903, pp. 79, 344.

10. Where used, it denotes either the theocracy or God's universal 'Kingship' over the world—almost as in the later Christian Fathers and in Thomas Aquinas!

11. See E. F. Scott, *The Kingdom of God in the New Testament,* 1931, ch. i, on the old Semitic and Persian conceptions; also H. Gressmann, *Der Messias,* 1929, who traces in bk. vii the development of a messianic expectation even in ancient Egypt. (It must be noted that not all Egyptologists agree to his interpretations.) For the old oriental and especially Persian background of the idea of the reign of the 'Great King', see F. W. Buckler, *The Epiphany of the Cross,* 1938; also my (now more or less 'dated') 'The Gospel of the Kingdom', in *The Biblical World,* l. 3 (Sept. 1917), esp. pp. 158f.

12. Cf. M. Dibelius, *The Message of Jesus Christ,* p. 21.

13. As in Canon Liddon's famous Bampton Lectures!

14. See my article, 'The Spiritual Christ', in the *Journal of Biblical Literature,* liv. 1 (March, 1935), pp. 1-15; *Frontiers of Christian Thinking,* 1935, chh. ii-iii.

15. See his (unfortunately still untranslated) *Die Messianischen Vorstellungen des jüdischen Volkes im Zeitalter der Tannaiten,* Berlin, 1904.

16. See H. J. Cadbury, *The Peril of Modernizing Jesus,* 1937 —a book that deserves to be read and re-read and laid to heart by all students of the New Testament.

17. *The Proposal of Jesus,* Doran, 1921.

CHAPTER VII

The Gospel in the New Testament

1. As Dibelius calls them; see his *Message of Jesus Christ*, Eng. tr. 1939, pp. 135-147.

2. See Karl Kundsin, in my *Form Criticism: A New Method of New Testament Research*, 1934, p. 84. Only in a very general way can anything be said of the *chronological* sequence of these 'strata'; perhaps for this reason 'strand' would suggest a better figure than 'stratum'. In translating Kundsin I used the word 'level'.

3. *Foundations: A Statement of Christian Belief in Terms of Modern Thought*, by Seven Oxford Men, 1913, p. 160; the quotation within the quotation is from T. R. Glover, 'The Death of Christ', a Student Christian Movement address delivered in 1912 and printed in *Christ and Human Need*.

4. They were 'church books' from the beginning. See my *Growth of the Gospels*, 1933, ch. i.

5. See Vladimir Simkhovitch, *Toward the Understanding of Jesus*, new ed. 1937, esp. ch. viii.

6. *The Proposal of Jesus*, 1921.

7. See E. F. Scott, *The First Age of Christianity*, 1926, p. 68.

8. See especially his books, *The Parables of the Kingdom*, 1935, rev. ed. 1936, *The Apostolic Preaching and Its Developments*, 1936, and *History and the Gospel*, 1938; also his lecture, 'The Gospels as History: a Reconsideration', published in the *Bulletin of the John Rylands Library*, xxii. 1 (Apr. 1938). See also the thorough critique by Professor Clarence Craig, 'Realized Eschatology', in the *Journal of Biblical Literature*, lvi. 1 (March 1937), pp. 17-26. There is a finely balanced appraisal of the whole question in an earlier work, E. F. Scott's *The Kingdom of God in the New Testament*, 1931, ch. ii.

9. *The Parables of the Kingdom*, p. 44.

10. In his little book, *Jesus*, 1939 (Sammlung Göschen, vol. 1130), esp. ch. vi.

11. See J. Hempel in *Record and Revelation*, ed. by H. W. Robinson, Oxford, 1938, esp. pp. 34, 56.

12. See A. N. Wilder, *Eschatology and Ethics in the Teaching of Jesus*, 1939.

13. Though the Christology of Q is not uniform, nor its usage of the term 'Son of Man'. Nor has the 'Son of Man' Christology even influenced all of Q. The relevant passages are fewer in number than is usually assumed—only seven, in Harnack's reconstruction of the source: Matt. 11:19 (probably editorial), 8:20 (perhaps originally a proverb), 12:39 (originally a self-reference, with a present verb rather than a future), 10:32 (also a self-reference, equivalent to 'I': certainly so understood by the first readers of Matthew), 12:32 (where the preceding verse, and the parallels, suggest that 'sons of men' or 'a son of man' was the original form), 24:44 and 24:27, 37, 39 (out and out apocalyptic, but generally acknowledged to be the formulation of the primitive Palestinian or Syrian church's expectations). One result of careful investigation is surely to modify the general impression that Q was dominated by a 'high' apocalyptic Christology of the Enochic type. Passages in Q reflecting other types of Christology are: Matt. 4:3, 6; 12:21; 11:3; 11:27; 23:34.

14. In *Christianity at the Cross-Roads*, 1909.

15. Mark certainly identifies his own 'Son of God' Christology (which is of course traditional) with the 'Son of Man' Christology already embedded in the tradition as it came to him.

16. For a good parallel to the attitude of such a military ruler as Pilate, see Pierre van Paassen's recent book, *Days of Our Years*, 1939, p. 149. Popular religious movements in the East are proverbially convertible overnight into dangerous political forces.

CHAPTER VIII

The Gospel and the Church

1. Let me refer once more to my article, 'The Spiritual Christ', in the *Journal of Biblical Literature*, liv. 1 (March 1935), pp. 1-15.

2. The Collect for the Feast of the Transfiguration, *Book of Common Prayer*, pp. 247f.

3. John 1:1, θεὸς ἦν ὁ λόγος. "Also ist auch von keiner Subordination die Rede, sondern der Λόγος wird mit Gott gleichgesetzt: er war Gott" (Bultmann, *Comm.*, 1937, p. 16). The old conjecture, θεῖος, 'divine', has never met with much favor by textual critics or exegetes.

4. See D. W. Riddle, 'Textual Criticism as a Historical Discipline', in the *Anglican Theological Review*, xviii (1936), pp. 220-233; also his recent work, *The Gospels, their Origin and Growth*, 1939, p. 81.

5. See W. von Baudissin, *Kyrios als Gottesname in Judentum*, 1929; C. H. Dodd, *The Bible and the Greeks*, 1935, ch. i; J. Weiss, *The History of Primitive Christianity*, i. 176, 250, ii. 741 note.

6. The argument set forth in the joint work by Lily Dougall and Cyril W. Emmet, *The Lord of Thought*, 1922, still deserves serious consideration.

7. See my article, 'The Church's Present Task', in *Religion in Life*, viii. 3 (1939), esp. pp. 346-349.

8. See B. H. Branscomb, *Jesus and the Law of Moses*, 1930; R. Knopf, *Einführung in das Neue Testament*, 3d ed. by H. Lietzmann and H. Weinel, Giessen, 1930, § 54.2.

9. Many scholars now hold that the apocalyptic passages in I-II Thessalonians are perhaps quoted from—or rest upon—some current apocalypse.

10. F. R. Barry, *The Relevance of the Church*, 1936, pp. 192, 202. See the whole chapter, indeed the whole book!

11. *Phaedo* 114e.